With your

Courage and Wisdom

You can Realize

Your Dream

Shail Sinha

This copy belongs to:

24 Heroic Journeys

Pathways of Ordinary People to Extraordinary Achievements

24 Heroic Journeys

Pathways of Ordinary People to Extraordinary Achievements

by Shall Sinha PhD

MENTOR
COMMUNICATIONS INC.
Edmonton, Alberta

Copyright © 1994 Mentor Communications Inc.

Cover design and text layout by Danie Hardie, Edmonton, AB.

ISBN 1-55056-276-2

Published by Mentor Communications Inc.
#200A 10130-103 Street, Edmonton, Alberta T5J 3N9

Canadian Cataloguing in Publication Data

Sinha, Shall, 1942
　　24 Heroic Journeys: Pathways of Ordinary People to
　　Extraordinary Achievements

ISBN 1-55056-276-2

1. Heros - Biography.　2. Heroines - Biography.　3. Courage.
I. Title.　II. Title. Twenty-four Heroic Journeys

CT105.S46 1994　　　　920.02　　　　C94-900163-5

Printed and bound in Canada by D. W. Friesen Printing.

TABLE OF CONTENTS

Reviews

This book is dedicated to Toastmasters International - the organization that gave me a new life.

Shall Sinha PhD

"*24 Heroic Journeys* provides inspirational and motivational reading. It's much like reading an executive summary of each extraordinary person's life"
    Frank C. Totino, P. Eng.

"*24 Heroic Journeys* is very interesting reading. It proves the old adage. If you think you can't, you won't. If you think you can, you will!"
    Alan MacLean, Rotarian

"It looks like a winner! It's a book sure to find interest, even with the busiest of people. Bite sized biographies everyone can enjoy."
    Grant Lovig, President of Company's Coming

"In our troubled world, leadership and influence guided by 'courage and wisdom' is particularly valuable. *24 Heroic Journeys* provides an ideal source for either a quick excursion or an extended exploration trip.
    Patrick Maguire, Superintendent of Schools, Sherwood Park Catholic Schools

"Great results come from inspired thought and concrete action. Nothing inspires like this collection of biographies. Give a copy of *24 Heroic Journeys* to someone you love. Start with yourself."
    Larry Anderson, President, Growth Marketing Inc.

"A world without heros is a wasteland: a desert without an oasis: a day without hope: a dreary place harbouring the myth of mankind's mediocrity. Shall Sinha tells us that it need not be that way. He has found his heros in the most diverse of places and, for that, we should all be grateful."
    Ron Collister, Journalist

Foreword

When Toastmasters International founder, Dr. Ralph C. Smedley was establishing the organization his vision was "To work together to bring out the best in each of us and to apply those skills to help others." Toastmasters International is now the largest self development organization in the world that is dedicated to the advancement of the individual. And it all started because one individual, Ralph Smedley, had the courage and wisdom to pursue his vision.

This book is about 24 individuals who overcame obstacles in their own lives to achieve extraordinary results and in the process helped countless others improve their lives. They may not have been members of Toastmasters International but they displayed some of the same core values that Dr. Smedley had set out to establish as the basis for his organization.

24 Heroic Journeys is also the result of another individual's vision. Shall Sinha is a dedicated Toastmaster member in Edmonton, Alberta. His vision was to write a book about great achievers with the idea that by reading about the pathways taken to extraordinary achievement, people may find inspiration to pursue greatness in themselves.

By putting that vision into action you may now take advantage of these short biographies to glean some insight to guide you on your own personal journey. In writing this book Shall Sinha has also carried on the vision of Ralph C. Smedley, 'developing his own skills and then using them to help others.'

I hope you enjoy this book and find some value in the experiences of these great individuals.

Neil R. Wilkinson, DTM
1993-94 President
Toastmasters International

About the Author

Shall Sinha was the second of 12 children of a family with very limited means. When he graduated with a degree in mechanical engineering, he was the first in the family to do so. He worked briefly in India as an assistant design engineer before coming to Canada for graduate studies. He arrived in Canada with 18 pounds of luggage, $8 in his pocket, and hardly knowing a soul on the continent. Becoming familiar with our climate, people, foods, customs and culture was a formidable challenge, but his prime concern was his ability to meet university standards for graduate students. What would he do if he failed? He had come with a one-way ticket!

He earned not only a Master's degree but also a PhD in engineering before becoming a specialist in aircraft vibration problems. Not satisfied with his academic achievements, he decided to pursue a Master of Business Administration (MBA) on a part-time basis. It was at that time that he was introduced to Toastmasters and became so enthralled by the field of personal development in general, and communications in particular, that he forgot about the MBA. From there, he got interested in the trait(s) that propel an ordinary person towards extraordinary achievements. *Heroic Journeys* is an introduction to the wealth of knowledge that he has accumulated during the last 10 years and over 15,000 hours of research.

Dr. Sinha writes in a conversational, plain-language style. In about five minutes of reading, you will absorb information that would normally require several hours of personal research. From this, you will benefit from the life lessons of an ordinary person who was able to overcome many obstacles to achieve extraordinary results!

If your group would like Dr. Sinha to present one of the stories from this book, or one of the over 500 such stories from his personal collection for your next conference, annual meeting or luncheon, please contact:

Mentor Communications Inc.
403•429•6342 or call Toll Free 1•800•4 MENTOR
or call Dr. Sinha directly at 403•467•8178.

Introduction

When I was a child, I heard my parents talk about Mahatma Gandhi as if he were an incarnation of God. In school, I read many stories about Gandhi's work and just could not believe how a man born in such lowly circumstances could become one of the greatest figures of his time. Later, I read the biographies of Abraham Lincoln and Benjamin Franklin and was intrigued to see the same apparent contradiction. Consequently, over the years, I read every biography I could lay my hands on.

I found inspiration in every one of them. I believed that the stories that touched me greatly might also touch others and thereby be a source of inspiration.

In business, there is a practice commonly referred to as OPM, ie. "Other People's Money." The idea is to borrow money from others, use it to develop your own business, return the borrowed money together with interest, and then keep the rest. In other words, you have used other people's money to build your own wealth. You can use the same idea to reach a chosen goal. Just like OPM, you can use OPE - Other People's Experience.

Life takes time and as such, it takes time to gain experience. The exciting thing is that every biography is a record of OPE! By reading biographies, we can accumulate a great deal of knowledge about OPE and then use these ideas to reach whatever goal we have set for ourselves. That is why I love to read biographies about extraordinary achievers.

I have spent numerous "few minutes" of my time waiting for doctors, lawyers, dentists, chiropractors, business executives, principals, even barbers. Since I am not much interested in the magazines lying on their coffee tables, I have often wished for a short gem that I could devour in that few minutes. Because of this, I generally carry my own reading material. I knew, from my research, that comprehensive biographical sketches were a rarity, so with the idea of providing people with a way to use the precious time in a reception area to gain valuable insight into other people's experience, I decided to write short biographies on ordinary people who have accomplished extraordinary feats.

As I wrote those mini-biographies, I also shared some of them with the audiences to whom I spoke and noted that almost everyone seemed to be touched by them. Many told me that they wanted copies of them, and some even suggested that I publish at least a few stories right away. Overwhelmed by the response and pressed by many requests, I decided to write this book as an introduction to an expanded work. Every story presented in this collection is the story of a heroic journey. Every story is thought-provoking, informative, and inspiring. To further enhance the appeal of the book, I have provided the added dimension by including artwork by Alberta artists. Although I have not provided detailed biographies of the artists, they too are ordinary people who have also demonstrated significant achievements.

As I have mentioned earlier, the stories included in this book are a sampling of my total research involving hundreds of biographies. These samples were chosen on the basis of not widely known facts of the early struggles of the persons and are presented in alphabetical order. I have presented each biography in chronological order to give you a sense of how the person's life progressed from conquering adversity to achieving the extraordinary. Should you wish to delve more deeply into the lives of the subjects, a reference is listed at the end of each story. This book is an excellent gift for any occasion and may spark new hope in the recipient.

I hope you enjoy the stories, and I wish you success in pursuing your dreams, whatever they may be.

Shall Sinha

Fringe Benefits, acrylic on canvas, Renee LaFontaine

Phineas Taylor Barnum 1

The Father of "the Greatest Show on Earth"

1810 - 1891

One can't think about P.T. Barnum without also thinking about the enterprise for which he is best known: the Barnum & Bailey Circus, heralded as The Greatest Show on Earth. Among the many talents that took Barnum to the pinnacle of the entertainment world were creativity, shrewdness, and a devotion to turning almost anything he did into dollars.

Phineas Taylor Barnum was born on July 5, 1810, in Bethel, Connecticut, the oldest of five children of a farming family. From his grandfather, he learned thrift. From the rest of his Puritan family, he learned to accept hard work as both a religious duty and a practical necessity.

When Barnum was a boy of 12, his father purchased the stock of a general store and appointed him clerk. There the boy learned to drive hard bargains. When he was 15 his father died, leaving the family bankrupt, so Barnum's personal savings were used up to pay the creditors. He even had to borrow money to buy a pair of shoes for his father's funeral. Having

managed to find a job as a clerk in a general store, he started exercising his bargaining skills. Sometime later, he set-up a lottery business in which he had great success, but it wasn't long before he returned to general store duties, securing another job, this time in Brooklyn, as a clerk in a store owned by distant relatives. Living above the store, his wake-up call for the day was a piece of rope tied to his leg which the night watchman tugged on at the first sign of a customer.

Encouraged by his success as a general merchant, he decided to open his own store. He returned to his home town and became the proprietor of a fruit and candy store. On its very first day in business, Barnum made back almost his entire investment. Slowly he enlarged his business by adding fancy goods to his stock and, at the same time, became an agent for a statewide lottery.

Having set a direction for his life, he married, built a two and a half storey home for his bride, a three-storey building for his general store, and some rental apartments. He also opened lottery offices in several towns where he developed and experimented with many creative ways of advertising lottery tickets. In doing so, he became the first person to use advertising and publicity campaigns to stir people's imaginations and interest in his business projects.

When he was 21, Barnum started a weekly newspaper in which he criticized anything that he thought took away people's liberties or any action that he considered unjust. He made a lot of enemies and even spent some time in jail, after being found guilty of libel. Nevertheless, after his release he continued to publish his paper. Two years later, he had to turn it over to his brother-in-law because of financial difficulties. He had been too generous in extending credit to his customers and the state of Connecticut had outlawed lotteries. At the age of 24, he sold everything he owned and moved to New York City with his wife and newborn daughter, just in time to see much of the city destroyed by fire. More than 700 buildings were gutted. Many companies went out of business. Banks could not pay their depositors and there were few opportunities to make money.

While visiting an exhibition, Barnum saw a woman who was supposed to be 161 years old and who, it was claimed, had been a nurse to George Washington. She was blind, toothless and crippled. It suddenly occurred to Barnum that he could make good money by exhibiting her! Thus he decided to "buy her". She was, in fact, "for sale", the asking price being $3,000. Barnum managed to bargain the price down to $1,000, of which he borrowed $500. It was a fateful turn for Barnum and for the world. He sold his interest in the general store to his partner and, with his new "exhibit," entered show business.

Using a variety of advertising techniques that he had developed himself, he was very successful and expanded his show by hiring a stunt man as well. The business folded when the old woman died and an autopsy revealed that she could not have been older than 80. Barnum joined a travelling circus and, after a year, he left it to start his own. Two years later, he again sold everything, this time to launch an investment scheme. He advertised that he had money to invest and received 93 responses, eventually forming a partnership for manufacturing several useful consumer items. The company prospered at first, but a year and a half later, it went broke, resulting in huge debts. To pay his creditors, he decided to go on the road again. He sent his family back home and formed a small entertainment company. For eight months he toured, but had only moderate success. Then, with his entire savings of $500, he bought 500 copies of Sears' Pictorial Illustrations of the Bible and opened an office in New York City to market them. He advertised widely and within six months had sold several thousand copies. Encouraged by this success, he opened branch offices in other cities and hired agents to handle sales. Unfortunately, most of his agents cheated him and he lost not only all his profits but also his original investment.

Once again he was broke. To earn a living, he wrote theatre advertisements and articles for Sunday papers and bought a museum with almost no down payment. Once again, he worked hard and used many creative ways to attract the public, one of which, was the use of bright calcium lights across the top of his building. Those early spotlights were the first ones seen in New York City. To entice more visitors, he instituted a variety of contests, such as the most beautiful baby, the fattest baby, the handsomest twins, the loveliest triplets, and so on. He spent all his waking hours thinking of ways to make the public more interested in his museum, enlarging his collections and making his exhibits more entertaining. Within a year, he had paid all of his loans and owned the museum outright.

By chance, he met a five-year-old boy one day who was only 23 inches tall and persuaded the boy's parents to sign a contract to exhibit him in Barnum's museum. He called the boy General Tom Thumb and claimed that he was 11 years old and had just arrived from England. Barnum soon flooded New York City with advertisements and billboards and was so successful that a year later, the two were able to tour Europe. Barnum hired tutors to teach the boy witty answers for any questions he was asked. They were in Europe for three years, visiting Queen Victoria three times, (once to accept a large payment in gold) and meeting the King of France. Later, Barnum found other dwarfs and created a variety of shows. By 38, he was admired as the world's greatest showman. For a while he settled down, enjoying semi-retirement, but it was not long before he accepted the challenge of promoting Jenny Lind, the Swedish Nightingale, and was once again very successful. His autobiography followed this success.

But just as success was not far away from P.T. Barnum, neither was disaster. At age 45, he was swindled so badly that he lost everything and had to move his family to a rented house in New York City while he set out on the road again. Five years after the latest bankruptcy, he was able to pay off his debts. Then his museum burned down. He rebuilt it next door, but that, too, was destroyed by fire, as was his next venture, which was a zoological garden.

At the age of 60, he decided to get back into the circus business. With two partners, he opened the Great Travelling World's Fair. As usual, with his advertising techniques and his enthusiasm, he developed it into a huge show.

Most of the major attractions that we find in a circus today were introduced by him in the late 1870s. Very soon, Barnum's show was so big that it was competing with the Bailey circus, the largest in the world at the time. Instead of trying to compete, he decided to join them. They merged and became the Barnum & Bailey Circus, which was later called The Greatest Show on Earth.

P.T. Barnum died on April 8, 1891 at the age of 81.

For more information on his life, see *The Life of P. T. Barnum*, by P.T. Barnum, revised edition, 1890; or *The Greatest Showman on Earth* by Ann Tompert, Dillon Press, Inc., Minneapolis, 1987.

Celadon Tea, watercolour, Vivian Thierfelder

Clara Barton 2

"Angel of the Battlefield"

1821 - 1912

The principal founder of the American Red Cross, was born on December 25, 1821, in North Oxford, Massachusetts. Her father owned a sawmill and had served in the Indian wars. Being the 5th and last child, and having siblings at least 10 years older than her, Clara was raised as though she were an only child and became accustomed to getting her own way. On the other hand, she enjoyed taking responsibility from an early age and when one of her brothers was bedridden for two years by a construction accident, he insisted that only Clara take care of him. This is how Clara Harlowe Barton began her destiny.

At the age of 15 and without any experience, she opened a school for workers and their children near her father's mill. After teaching there for 15 years, she decided to go back to school, eventually graduating and taking a teaching position in Bordentown, New Jersey. Noting that the town did not have any free public school, and that many young people just walked the streets or loitered, she offered to teach for

three months, without pay, on the condition that the town make the school free for everyone. At first, the town council refused but finally yielded to her persistence. Starting with six students, she had more than 600 within two years!

Impressed by the success of that experiment, but believing that the task of running such a school would be too much for a woman who was barely five feet tall, the town appointed a man as principal. Insulted, Barton resigned immediately. She then found a clerical job in the patent office in Washington, D.C. with the help of her Republican Congressman. She thus became one of the first women to hold a full-time position as a civil servant. Even though the men in the office resented her, she hung on, impressing her superiors with her efficiency. When the Democrats won the next election, she lost her job and did not work in Washington for four years, at which time she was rehired following the victory of Abraham Lincoln.

When the Civil War broke out, Barton decided to

get involved. She adopted the motto "What is no-body's business is my business" and on her own, collected supplies such as bandages, medicines, food, and tobacco, announcing that she would personally deliver them to the battlefield. Although it was highly irregular for a woman to visit the front, she persisted and, once there, arranged to have several hundred loaves of bread baked for breakfast, soup served from laundry tubs and coffee ladled to soldiers by the gallon. Next, she turned her attention to nursing the wounded, sometimes where they fell. Many times she risked her life. On one occasion, just as she raised a soldier's head so that he could sip from a cup, a bullet whizzed between her body and her arm, hitting the soldier in the chest and killing him instantly. Her clothes were sometimes torn by flying bullets, but she refused to slow down. Because of her courage, the soldiers called her "the Angel of the Battlefield." After the war, she set up an organization for tracing missing soldiers. She identified the bodies of the war dead and notified their families. During her entire lifetime, her name was associated with the Bureau of Missing Men. "Ask Miss Barton" became a stock phrase.

From 1866 to 1868 she lectured in the Midwest, relating her wartime experiences and stories. Veterans, many of whom had survived because of her care, dotted the audiences, as did women in mourning. Her lecture work tired her even more than the battlefield, so much, that at one lecture she almost fainted. Her doctor told her to go to Europe for a rest, so in August 1869 she sailed for Switzerland. She never did get that rest. Soon after her arrival, she was introduced to a new project called the International Red Cross, which had been created by the Geneva Conference in 1864. When the Franco-Prussian war broke out, she stayed eight months in Strasbourg where she instituted sew-ing jobs for women, a project which not only saved the workers from penury but also clothed 30,000 people. She then moved to Paris where, for two months, she distributed money and clothing under the insignia of the International Red Cross.

After returning to the United States, she lobbied relentlessly to create the American Red Cross Society, gathering well-wishers and eager workers around her. She buttonholed reporters, diplomats, and generals. She made forays into key offices. She distributed leaflets everywhere. She approached the Secretaries of the Navy and the Treasury and the United States Postmaster General. She even approached the President of the United States.

President Hayes was not very supportive, but his successor, President Garfield, promised to help. Unfortunately, he died before he could do anything for her, and his successor, President Arthur, was less enthusiastic. Finally, following one of her talks, the ex-President of Yale University, Dr. Theodore D. Woolsey, publicly announced his strong support for the cause. Encouraged by that support, Barton started developing the Constitution of the Red Cross. It was approved in Washington on May 21, 1881. On March 1, 1882, after more than 10 years of lobbying, the American Red Cross was chartered and Clara Barton became its first president. She devoted all her time to its operation, refused to accept any salary and even spent her own savings when public contributions failed to cover the organization's costs. Even in her seventies, she continued to work hard on many projects, including helping the victims of the great Johnstown flood in Pennsylvania, the survivors of Turkey's massacre of Armenians, and the victims of a hurricane that devastated parts of Georgia.

By the end of 1897, she had settled down on a

farm at Glen Echo, Maryland, but a year later, at the age of 77, she was off again serving in the Spanish-American War. She personally rode to the battlefield on a mule-driven wagon to help the Cuban civilians and the American soldiers. She set up orphanages for Cuban children, served soup to the soldiers and treated wounds. In 1902, at the Seventh International Red Cross Conference, she was acclaimed. Later that year, President Theodore Roosevelt had her by his side on the reviewing stand at the Spanish American War Veterans Convention in Detroit.

By the age of 83, her work with the organization became sporadic, while the Red Cross administration had become highly organized. She formally resigned her presidency on May 4, 1904, and died on April 12, 1912, at the age of 90.

For more information on her life, see *Clara Barton: The Angel of the Battlefield*, by Rae Bains, Troll Associates, 1982.

Headmaster, brush and ink on paper, Wayne McGale

Edward Bok 3

"Architect of the Ladies Home Journal"

1863 - 1930

A publisher and moral crusader, Edward Bok was born on October 9, 1863 in the Netherlands. At the age of seven, his father lost all his money in a business venture and decided to migrate to the United States. The family settled in Brooklyn, New York. While he was in grammar school, Edward helped to support the family by working twice a week cleaning windows in a bakery. He also delivered papers and sold icewater and lemonade.

When he was but 12 years old, he attended a party and wrote a story about it. In this story he included the names of everyone who had been there. Taking his story to the publisher of the local newspaper, he pointed out that every name in the report meant one extra sale for the paper. The publisher bought his column and asked him to submit two more columns every week.

At 13, Bok heard that Western Union, where his father worked, had an opening for an office boy. He applied, got the job, and quit school forever. To continue his education, he took evening courses and read books borrowed from the public library. He also bought a copy of *Appleton's Encyclopaedia* and began studying the lives of famous people. Out of curiosity he wrote a letter to President James A. Garfield, asking him to verify some information he had read. Garfield sent him a warm, personal reply which tickled the boy enough that he wrote to a number of his heroes asking about different events in their lives. Every one of them sent a personal reply. Very soon, Bok had a collection of autographed letters. Next, he began watching the local papers for announcements about the visits of distinguished people to New York City, and after they arrived, he would call them for an interview. In that way, he made friends with General and Mrs. Grant, General Sherman, Mrs. Abraham Lincoln, Jefferson Davies, and many others.

One day, he noticed a man throw away a picture from a package of cigarettes. He picked it up and wondered why such a beautiful picture was simply discarded. Immediately, the idea struck him that a short biography of that person would enhance the value of the picture, so he called the publisher of the pictures with his idea. He was asked to select some famous people and write a 200-word biography on each. The idea proved to be so popular that Bok had to hire three people to do the necessary research.

Bok built on both his creative talent and his connections. When he became the editor of a local church paper, it lept to national prominence overnight because it contained articles by the nation's most famous people. They had written because of their personal friendship with Edward. He learned to take shorthand and found a job as a stenographer in a publishing company. He attended lectures by famous people and reported on them for his paper. When he could not write down everything, he called on the person for a private interview, and in that way, made more friends.

He then organized the Bok Syndicate Press which distributed materials to newspapers all over the country. Bok noticed that there wasn't much material of interest to women in any publications, so he began a women's page. That was a pioneering step. Until that time, publishers did not include any material for women because women generally did not read the papers. Bok reasoned that women did not read the papers because there was nothing in the papers for them to read, consequently, his women's page proved his argument by becoming very popular. It became so popular, in fact, that it caught the attention of Cyrus Curtis, the publisher of *Ladies' Home Journal*. Curtis travelled to New York City and invited Bok to become the editor of his magazine. At the time, that appeared to be a big gamble. Bok had a good position with a well-established publisher, Scribner and Sons, while

Ladies' Home Journal was a little known publication and, to date, there was not one successful women's magazine on the market. His friends advised him against the move, but Bok saw it as a challenge. He accepted the offer and moved to Philadelphia.

Over the years, he introduced many new features and invited readers to write and tell him what they liked and disliked about the magazine. He engaged a specialist to start a child care column. He bought stories from many highly respected writers. He persuaded the daughters of well-known men to write their personal recollections of their fathers. He hired an architect to design a series of attractive, low-priced houses and sold the floor plans and building specifications to his readers at a nominal price. He ran photographs of tastefully decorated homes and started a page called "Good Taste and Bad Taste." That feature forced American furniture manufacturers to think about such factors as comfort and good looks which, until then, had been generally ignored.

In 1889, when he took over as editor, *Ladies' Home Journal* had about 40,000 readers. Five years later, the circulation was well over a million, soon climbing to 2 million. Bok then turned his attention to social reforms, writing an article criticizing women's clubs. He condemned their programs, creating a large number of enemies overnight. Many women threatened to sue him. But instead of being defensive, he took strong offensive action, advising his company lawyer to start legal proceedings against the executives of the clubs and to notify their husbands about his intentions. He wrote several articles explaining why he thought their work had been totally useless. Within a week, the husbands of every executive member wrote back, pleading him to drop the case. He then started publishing what he thought they should be doing and some of the members even appreciated his help.

Bok soon broadened his social criticism. He spoke against the custom of women wearing the plumes of shorebirds in their hair. He argued that the plumes, called aigrettes, came from nesting female herons and similar birds. The mother birds were killed to get the plumes, and their babies were left to starve. When no one seemed to pay any attention to him, he wrote to legislators, and within a few months, a law prohibiting aigrettes was passed in several states. A little later, Congress made the importation of aigrettes a federal offence.

In 1892, he announced that the *Ladies' Home Journal* would not accept any advertisements for patent medicines. He had become convinced that the formulas that the medicine companies said would cure cancer, ulcers, skin diseases and "female complaints" did nothing of the sort, and in fact, made addicts of those who used the medication and caused pregnant women who took the compounds to give birth to unhealthy babies. The struggle went on for a long time, with Bok finally hiring a young lawyer to make a detailed investigation. The result was an article called *"The Great American Fraud."* He became instrumental in the passage of the nation's first Pure Food and Drug Act. Bok also campaigned against the unsightly billboards that lined the railroad tracks, obscuring the landscapes and assaulting travellers' eyes with advertisements for soap, tonic, or chewing tobacco. As a result of his efforts, hundreds of billboards were torn down, yet his magazine never lost a single advertiser. Lastly, he started a column called *"Dirty Cities,"* in which he presented factual accounts of the filth to be found in America's cities. The column resulted in many cities cleaning their slums and be-

coming more pleasant and attractive to live in.

After 30 years of service as the editor of *Ladies' Home Journal*, Edward Bok retired and turned to the task of writing his autobiography. Entitled *The Americanization of Edward Bok*, the book won a Pullitzer Prize for biography.

Bok died in 1930 at the age of 67.

For more information on his life, see *The Americanization of Edward Bok*, 1921.

Spanish Charm, acrylic on canvas, Elizabeth Bowering

Carol Burnett 4

"From One-room Apartment to National Celebrity"

Born in 1933

Comedian Carol Burnett was born on April 26, 1933, in San Antonio, Texas. She arrived in California at the age of seven, but not to live in a Hollywood mansion or even to seek stardom. Her parents had left Texas five years before, leaving Carol in her grandmother's care. Both of her parents were drinkers and her father could not hold down a job. They separated in California where Carol's mother lived on welfare just down the street from Carol and her grandmother. Carol's living quarters, at that time, consisted of a one-room apartment with no closets and one bed that pulled down from the wall. There she lived for 14 years.

The family lived on welfare, which meant poverty and hand-me-down clothes. The one luxury Carol could enjoy was movies. She and her grandmother loved to go to the movies in the many nearby theaters. They went in the afternoon when movies were the cheapest; they cost all of 11 cents per person. Sometimes she saw as many as eight movies a week. After a

movie, she and her friends would sometimes act out the scenes and in the privacy of her tiny apartment, she liked to pretend she was an announcer for a radio station. One day someone yelled, "Turn that radio down," This convinced her that she could act. She also played elaborate pranks on her friends, telling one of them that she had a twin sister named Karen. For nearly six months, she played the two roles and got away with it.

She didn't pursue what might have seemed like an obvious career choice. Her grandmother wanted her to take secretarial training, while her mother thought she should write, mainly because she felt that Carol was quite ugly. Carol enjoyed writing, so she decided to take up journalism. The tuition fee at the university was $42, more than their monthly rent, so higher education seemed out of the question. Then one day, she found in her mail box an envelope addressed to her containing a fifty-dollar bill. There was no note, and she never knew who gave her that money, but she used it to enroll at the University of California at Los Angeles. There was no journalism school there, so she enrolled in a theater arts program. In her first play there, she was supposed to be a waitress, but it never occurred to her to read the whole play. She memorized only her own part and received failing grades for her effort.

By her third year, she had improved markedly and was invited to participate in a program for faculty members and their guests. After the performance, an elderly man asked her and another student, Don, what their plans were. Both said they would go to New York if they had the money. The man asked them to come to his office and there he presented them with $1,000 each. " But," he told them, "There are some conditions. This is not a gift. This is a loan. There is no interest on it. You must return this money in exactly five years. You must use this money only for going to New York and for pursuing your acting career. You must never reveal my name and when you become financially successful, you must help some other person in the same way that I am helping you today." Carol had never seen that much money in her life. She left for New York City right away; Don was to follow her later.

She found New York City strange and very expensive. Fortunately, she was able to join a group called the Rehearsal Club which was a cheap place for girls to stay while they looked for acting work. Although she pounded the sidewalk day and night, no door opened to her, until finally, one agent said, "Let me know when you are performing next. I will come and watch you."

"But how do I perform if no one gives me a chance?", she asked.

"That's easy," he said. "Put on a show yourself".

She, Don and 23 girls decided to do just that. They each chipped in 25 cents a night for the rehearsal space and worked hard to sell enough tickets to pay for the rental of the theater. Finally, on March 3, 1955, they performed to a packed house. The show was very successful. Every girl got some kind of job, but Carol Burnett proved to be the star of the night. As a result, she found an agent and more work. On December 17, 1955, she made her first national television appearance, singing love songs to a puppet on *The Paul Winchell Show*. On the same day, she and Don were married. The marriage lasted for a little more than four years. Don struggled with his career and felt uncomfortable with his wife's successes.

In 1956, Burnett appeared on *Stanley*, a weekly series, and that same fall she also appeared on *The Garry Moore Show*. For three years, she was a frequent guest on that show and then became " a regular". She was now in a position to help her family, and in December of 1957, she brought her stepsister Chrissy to live with her. Her parents had both died by this time, but she moved her grandmother to a bigger apartment, where she lived until her death in 1967. On June 22, exactly five years from the date she had received it, Carol returned the $1,000.00 loan.

In 1962, she left The *Garry Moore Show* to work on her own, appearing with Julie Andrews on a TV special, *Julie and Carol at Carnegie Hall*. That was the first production of Carol's million-dollar, 10-year contract with CBS. While working with *The Garry Moore Show*, she had fallen in love with its producer, Joe Hamilton, who was separated from his wife and eight children. They were married in 1963 and had three daughters. Although she was far happier with Joe than she had been with Don, the marriage fell apart 19 years later.

In September 1967, production of *The Carol Burnett Show* began. The show ran until August 1978 for a total of 286 episodes, including over 1,500 comedy sketches and 500 musical numbers. It became one of the most popular television programs of all time. Burnett also appeared in several movies, including *Pete 'n' Tillie*, *Friendly Fire* and *Annie*. A 1977 poll revealed that she was one of the world's 20 most admired women and in several subsequent polls, she was voted the most popular all-round female entertainer.

For more information on her life, see *Carol Burnett*, by David Paige, Creative Education, 1977.

Making Memories, acrylic on canvas, Jo Petterson

Andrew Carnegie 5

"From Bobbin Boy to Multi-Millionaire"

1835 - 1919

A combination of shrewdness and determination enabled Andrew Carnegie to become the backbone of the American steel industry in the late 19th century, as well as, one of the richest men in America.

Carnegie was born on November 25, 1835, in Dunfermline, Scotland, the son of a handloom weaver. When he was 13, he moved with his family to Allegheny, Pennsylvania, a suburb of Pittsburgh. A year later, he found a job in a cotton factory filling bobbins. At 15, he became a telegraph messenger boy. He was very conscious of making the best use of every minute of his time, so while he waited for telegraph messages to deliver, he read, borrowing books faithfully every Saturday night from a man in Pittsburgh. He read the plays of William Shakespeare and the poetry of Robert Burns. Although he did not believe in God, he read the Bible carefully because he thought it an important book. He also read about the ancient Greeks and Romans. Before long, he was writing letters to the *New York Tribune* about political issues, especially slavery, which he detested.

By watching the telegraph operators, he learned telegraphy and by 16 he, too, was a telegraph operator. Over the next two years, his work so impressed Thomas Scott, the division superintendent of the Pennsylvania Railroad, that Scott hired him as his private secretary and personal telegrapher. As Scott moved up, he fostered Carnegie's promotion as well, and six years later, Carnegie was the superintendent of the Pittsburgh division. When the Civil War broke out, Carnegie assisted Scott in military telegraphy and transportation for the Union Army.

Under Scott's guidance, Carnegie began investing his savings in stocks, small amounts at first and then more and more, ever enlarging his modest portfolio. Within a very short time, he was very wealthy. When the Civil War ended, he was just under 30 years old, still small and boyish-looking but possessing great foresight. Reasoning that rebuilding the nation would generate a great deal of business activities, he quit his railroad job and devoted himself full-time to building his own business. He invested in Adam Express Company Stock, bought a one-eighth interest in a sleeping car company, and invested in oil lands in western Pennsylvania. He also invested heavily in the rapidly expanding iron industry, building great iron and steel works in Pittsburgh.

At the age of 16, he had earned $200 a year; by 33 he was making $50,000. Between 1867 and 1873, he sold more than $30 million in bonds, earning substantial commissions. At that point, he wrote a note to himself stating that in just two more years he would have enough money to retire, at which point he would attend Oxford University in England to get a sound education. With that background, he would buy a newspaper and be active in public affairs for the rest of his life. But life was to take him in a different direction. During a business trip to England in 1872, he learned about a new way of making steel. Becoming so excited about the future of the steel business, he decided to abandon all other business interests, and put all of his eggs in one basket, making/selling steel. He then set about to tend to that basket. He bought the best ore lands he could find near Lake Superior. He built his own fleet of ships to carry iron from the mines to his furnaces. He bought coalfields. By 1888, he was chief owner of Homestead Steel Works and controlled other large steel companies.

His success was sometimes marred by personal tragedy with the year 1886 being the saddest in his life. In the fall, he took his mother to their summer home in Cresson, hoping that the mountain air and scenery would help restore her failing health, but soon he was stricken with typhoid. His younger brother, Tom, who came to visit them, developed a sudden case of pneumonia and died. His mother's death

followed shortly thereafter. For a while, Andrew lost all interest in living. To regain his health, he started riding, often accompanied by a companion, Louise Whitfield. Eventually, he fell in love with her, and they married in April 1887. He was 52; she was 29.

At heart, Carnegie was an optimist, especially in matters of business. This characteristic was an important reason for his success. Even in hard times in the United States, particularly during the depressions of 1873 and 1893, he remained confident that the nation would recover. Even when prices were low, he kept all his workers at their jobs, bought new equipment, improved his buildings, and watched every penny. Consequently, when prosperity returned, he could sell steel cheaper than any of his rivals. Between 1875 and 1900, he dropped his prices from $160 a ton to $17 a ton and still took home a profit.

By 1900, Carnegie was the master of the United States steel industry. He could make steel at a lower cost than anyone in America or Europe, and he had helped establish America as the largest producer of steel in the world. It was steel that made America the leader among all the world's industrial nations. In 1901, two years after organizing his vast steel interests into the Carnegie Steel Company, he sold his enterprise to the United States Steel Corporation and retired from business. For the next 20 years, he did what he most enjoyed, reading, travelling, listening to fine music, collecting art, writing books, and giving money away. He believed that a wealthy man had an obligation to use his fortune to create opportunity for all and to increase knowledge. Most of his gifts went to support education, public libraries and world peace. By 1915, he had given away more than $300 million. In addition to providing funds for more than 2,500 library buildings, he established the Carnegie

Foundation for the Advancement of Teaching and the Carnegie Institute of Washington, D.C. He also pioneered the concept of the Master Mind Alliance and put together a group consisting of approximately 50 men.

After a long and colourful career, Andrew Carnegie died on August 9, 1919, at the age of 83. In 1976 he was listed in the American Hall of Fame.

For more information on his life, see *Andrew Carnegie*, by Clara Ingram Judson, Follett Publishing Co., 1964; or *Andrew Carnegie* by Joseph Frazier Wall, Oxford University Press, New York, 1970.

Quadra Island Woman, acrylic on masonite, Katherine Fraser

Emily Carr 6

"The Artist, Decades Ahead of Her Time"

1871 - 1945

One of Canada's greatest artists was born on December 13, 1871, in Victoria, British Columbia, the second youngest of five daughters of a wholesale grocer. As a child, Emily Carr struggled to sit still at a desk. She much preferred to be outside playing in the country fields and woods. She loved to sit on the woodpile in the barnyard and sing. She loved animals and often, to get away from all her scolding elders, she would ride her pony into the countryside.

In school, she was an average student but showed special ability in drawing. Impressed by her talent, her father allowed her to take art classes, and she made an easel by tying branches from a cherry tree snugly together. When she was 12, her mother died, and she found herself alone much of the time. For the most part, her family did not encourage her artistic ability. Nevertheless, she was able to set up her own studio in the loft of the barn where she gave lessons in painting.

She taught at the Ladies' Art Club of Vancouver, but her critiques proved to be too radical for the students there, and she was dismissed. She taught children's art classes as well. In this, she was more successful and so was able to save money to visit Indian villages and eventually travel to France. Her instructor in France, Harry Gibb, taught her how to express mood in her paintings by using contrasting colours without worrying about whether the colours were true to life or not.

Against her family's wishes, she left teaching to study art in London, San Francisco, and Paris, remaining abroad for several years. In 1910, some of her paintings were exhibited in Paris. When she returned home, she tried to exhibit her paintings in Canada, but people did not like them. Just about everyone thought she was eccentric in trying to devise a style that reflected what she felt rather than what she saw. Her originality and use of colour set her completely apart from other artists of the time. Her family considered her a disgrace and refused to discuss her paintings in their home. Schools in which she had previously taught, now refused to hire her. The private students whom she had tutored before leaving for Europe, left her. Destitute and alone, she wondered whether painting was worth the trouble it was causing her, but she refused to give up. Instead, she packed her camping equipment and painting supplies and went to visit some of her Indian friends. She was determined to paint the British Columbia forests in her own special way, even if others neither liked nor understood her work.

Deeply discouraged and unable to earn a living from either painting or teaching, she decided to convert the house she had inherited into a boarding house and devote her remaining time to painting. She rented as much space as she could and lived in a room so small that there was no space for a chair for a visitor. She designed a pulley system and hung two chairs from the ceiling. When a guest arrived, she simply lowered one of the chairs. When she had more than two visitors, they had to chat without sitting down. But cooking, washing and cleaning left her little time for painting, and the works that she displayed in her own house were loudly ridiculed, even by her tenants. No one encouraged her work. She was often seen wheeling an old-fashioned baby carriage with her pet monkey inside or walking with a number of big, shaggy sheepdogs which she raised to sell. During the 22 years that she ran her boarding house, which she called the House of All Sorts, she did so little painting that she lost almost all interest in it.

To relieve her despair, she often returned to the woodlands where she developed an attachment to the Indian people. She admired their honesty, knowledge of nature, and forthright personalities. They seemed to mirror the direct and truthful reactions that she had tried to capture on canvas. The Indians loved her ever present sense of humour. Laughter, often at her own expense, had become her only means of assuaging her disappointment. The Indians gave her a new name, Klee Wyck, which means, "the laughing one." They also loved her paintings of the totem poles in the natural settings of the British Columbia forests. At the time, it seemed that the Indians were the only people who admired her art, and it was through some of them that word of her extraordinary ability as a painter reached the higher circles in Ottawa.

One day, a representative from the National Gallery of Canada called to see some of her paintings. She was reluctant to bring them out because she thought he would just make fun of them, but she allowed him to see them, and he asked her for permission to display them in Ottawa. He also agreed to pay her expenses to visit Ottawa for the exhibition. Delighted, she accepted his offer. On her way to Ottawa, she stopped in Toronto and visited Eric Brown, one of the members of the Group of Seven. She discovered that their ideas were very similar, so on her way home from Ottawa, she stopped in Toronto once again, this time, to see Lawren Harris. She was very impressed by his work and resolved to get back to her painting.

Soon after her return from Ottawa, the Art Gallery of Toronto purchased three of her old paintings for $1,000. Then the Vancouver Art Gallery bought a few. She was by now in her late fifties, and her paintings were suddenly in great demand. She regained her old passion for painting, returning to her easel with all her vigour and enthusiasm intact. She was also very careful not to be influenced by wealth. She had painted for the love of the forests and did not want to change that.

The House of All Sorts still demanded a lot of her

time, but she refused to work exclusively as a landlady. She walked into the woods, stared at the quiet forest, and slowly picked up her brush. She painted and painted. She bought a motorhome and spent the summer months in the woods. She loved pets, and they always accompanied her. The monkey often sat on her shoulder, restricting her ability to paint. Each day, she went deeper and deeper into the woods. To protect herself from the mosquitoes, she made a mask out of a net. Sometimes she would sit in the forest for hours to get a deeper sense of the feelings it evoked in her.

Old age and the rigours of a hard life in the forest slowly took their toll. Emily suffered a heart attack and became confined to her bed. With her doctor's permission, she began to write about her childhood, about her life in the woodlands, and about her painting. She sent her manuscript to a publisher, who not only rejected it but also lost it and consequently, did not return it until it was found a year later. She eventually published the same manuscript with the title *Klee Wyck*. To her surprise, it won the Governor General's award for non-fiction writing and immediately drew new interest in her paintings. She also wrote a book "on being small" and another called *The House of All Sorts*.

In 1941, after many difficult years, she finally found well deserved recognition when the city of Victoria gave her an official 70th birthday party. She enjoyed her last years, content that her paintings were being shown in exhibitions in Europe and North America. Emily Carr died in 1945, at the age of 74.

For more information on her life, see *Emily Carr*, by Marion Endicott, The Women's Press, Toronto; or *Emily Carr*, by Doris Shadbolt, Douglas & McIntyre, Vancouver, 1990.

Lonny, acrylic on canvas, Christina Saruk Reid

George Washington Carver 7

"The Peanut Scientist"

1864 - 1943

George Washington Carver had many talents, but he will be remembered for all time for his contributions to agriculture. His life was a long journey from the obscurity and degradation of slavery to a preeminent position as one of America's pioneer agriculturists.

No one knows George Washington Carver's exact date of birth, but it is believed to be the early part of 1864. His parents were slaves, and when he was just a baby, he and his mother were kidnapped in an Indian raid. He was later found abandoned in the bush, but his mother was never found. He was raised by his master, whose name 'Carver' he adopted. The Carvers were a kind couple, raising George as a member of their own family and teaching him how to cook, mend, and embroider. Because he was black, he was not allowed to enroll in the local school, but somehow he learned the alphabet, and more importantly he learned how to treat ailing plants, a skill which even then earned him a nickname, "the plant doctor."

When he was 12, the Carvers sent him to a school for black children in a nearby village. Here he lived with a childless black couple and was taught how to wash and iron clothes. Within a year, he had learned all that the school could offer him, so he joined a family that was moving to a bigger town. He arranged to live with a blacksmith in return for cooking meals and doing other household chores.

One day, Carver witnessed 30 masked men break into the town jail, drag out a black prisoner, beat him to death, and then hang his body on a lamppost and burn it. That was his first and most lasting experience of racial hatred.

He soon moved to another town, where he lived with another black couple, helping them with domestic chores while attending school. At the age of 16, he moved with his host family to Minneapolis, Kansas. There he opened his own laundry business and attended school with mostly white students. He also did some gardening and painting and played the accordion. In his school, there was another student with the same name as his, so he decided to add a middle initial. The letter W popped into his mind and he became known as George W. Carver. When his friends asked what the W stood for, he could not answer until one day a boy asked if it meant "Washington." He thought for a moment and replied, "Yes, why not?" and from that day his name became George Washington Carver.

When he was 21, he applied for admission to Highland College, a small religious school in the northeast corner of Kansas. Because of his marks, he was accepted, but when he arrived on campus, he was told that there has been a mistake. " We don't accept black students!" So for the next several years, he wandered through the farming areas of Kansas, working at odd jobs, until a white couple advised him to apply at Simpson College in Indiana. Here, he was accepted. He was 26 and the only black student on the college campus. He got along in the white community by keeping his feelings to himself and making friends through his hard work and many talents. To earn money while attending college, he set up a laundry in a shack close to the campus and registered for classes in grammar, arithmetic, essay writing, piano and singing. He also wanted to try art, but was rejected at first. However, he persisted and was finally permitted to enter the painting class.

Throughout his college career, Carver's obvious talent was in agriculture. He had demonstrated an extraordinary ability to raise, crossbreed, and graft plants, which brought him another nickname, this time the " Green Thumb Boy." On the suggestion of a teacher, he moved to Iowa State College to study agriculture, where once again, he was the only black student on campus. After overcoming some initial

distrust, he became one of the most popular students. He was active in prayer meetings, wrote the class poems, attended meetings of the college debating, German and art clubs, rose to the rank of captain in the Reserve Officers Training Corps, played the guitar, and even became a masseur. To support himself in Iowa, he did menial jobs but still found time for his favourite occupation, painting. During the 1893 World Columbian Exhibition in Chicago, one of his paintings won an honourable mention in competition with the world's best artists. But agriculture eclipsed his painting career by the time he was 30 and had earned him his bachelor's degree. At that point, he started working as an assistant botanist while studying for his master's degree.

In 1896, at the age of 32, he became the first black man in America to earn a graduate degree. He could have stayed at that university but was invited by Booker T. Washington, to set up the agriculture department at Tuskegee Institute in Alabama. In a letter to Carver, Booker wrote, "I cannot offer you money, position or fame. I offer you, in their place, work - hard, hard work - the task of bringing a people from degradation, poverty and waste to full manhood." He accepted the challenge and moved to Tuskegee.

For 47 years, until his death, he served at Tuskegee. He did not marry because he said he never had the time. Starting from scratch, he built his department into one of the most advanced agricultural schools in the country. Since the farmers and many others who needed his services could not come to him, he went to them. He taught the entire community how to grow better crops. Single-handedly, in his own laboratory, he developed over 300 different uses for peanuts. He taught farmers how to rotate crops and prepare rich fertilizers from everyday wastes. All the while he refused to take part in any "purely social" activity on the campus, living simply, dressing in shabby old clothes and letting his pay cheques mount up, uncashed, on his desk.

Although his laboratory made him world famous, he never enjoyed the respect that he deserved. He was never physically threatened but suffered many insults. For example, he was never able to dine at the scientific meetings he addressed and did not attend a Montgomery concert by Paderewski because blacks were not allowed in the theatre. When a pipe organ in Tuskegee was dedicated to him, he stayed home from the ceremony because it was held at a white church.

George Washington Carver died on January 5, 1943, at the age of 79. Thirty-five years later, in 1973, he was listed in the American Hall of Fame.

For more information on his life, see *George Washington Carver: The Man Who Overcame Obstacles*, by Lawrence Elliott, Prentice Hall, 1966.

Gallery Glads, watercolour, Cecile Derkatch

Ray Charles 8

"The Genius of Soul"
Born in 1930

Musician and composer, Ray Charles Robinson was born on September 23, 1930, in Albany, Georgia. His father was a railroad repairman, consequently, he was rarely around the house. His mother was a washerwoman and maid. When he was only a few months old, his family moved to Greenville, Florida.

His passion for music began at a very early age. From the moment he discovered that there were piano keys to be mashed, he started mashing them, trying to make sounds out of his feelings. When he was barely three years old, he tried to imitate the boogie-woogie played by the proprietor of Greenville's Redwing Cafe. He was also exposed to gospel music at the local Baptist church and to country music on the local radio stations.

When he was five years old, he saw his younger brother drown in a washtub. Soon after that, he started waking up in the morning with his eyes caked with mucous. His sight became increasingly blurred, and within two years he was totally blind. To ensure

that his blindness did not incapacitate him, his mother continued to give him household chores and to allow him to play outside with other children. She also sent him to a school for deaf and blind children where he learned to compose and arrange music in Braille and to play the piano, clarinet, alto saxophone, organ, and trumpet. His mother died when he was 15, probably of food poisoning, and afterwards, her son decided not to go back to school. His father's death from diabetes followed shortly thereafter. Ray left home and went to Jacksonville, where he stayed with family friends and earned his living by taking occasional jobs as a pianist in a combo or big band.

In 1946, at the age of 16, he moved to Orlando. Totally on his own and facing competition from dozens of hungry musicians, he too went hungry, at times being forced to survive on a diet of crackers and sardines. In spite of hardship, however, he refused to relinquish his hard-earned independence. From Orlando, he moved to Tampa, where he found a job with the Florida Playboys, which had been an all-white country and western band. Within a year, he had saved $600 and decided to move as far away as $600 could take him. He got on the bus in Orlando and rode it until he reached Seattle. A day after his arrival, he sang in a talent showcase at a club called Rocking Chair and was offered steady work. He formed a trio with two other musicians, and they performed in clubs all over Seattle, producing their first record, *Confession Blues* in 1948. Following these initial successes, he moved to Los Angeles in 1950 and dropped his surname to avoid confusion with the boxer Sugar Ray Robinson.

It was at about this time that Charles became addicted to heroin, but in spite of that, he continued to pursue his music and record his songs. He scored his first national hit with *Baby, Let Me Hold Your Hand*, which was released in 1951 and sold 100,000 copies over the next two years. He also began touring as a pianist, composer, and arranger with a blues band. Although he enjoyed considerable success, music critics compared his voice to that of Nat King Cole. Charles craved recognition of his own. During the mid '50s he literally lived on the road, touring the 'black' beer halls and honky-tonks known in the business as the Chitlin Circuit. He played and sang with any freelance musician in whatever town he happened to be in and continued to work on his voice. By 1954, he had formed his own seven-piece band, and Atlantic Records gave him free rein in their recording studio. That year, he recorded *I Got a Woman*, which became a smash hit and brought recognition for his unique style.

When he released *What I'd Say* in 1959, he began to attract a large following among whites as well as blacks. Despite having been banned by many

radio stations for its suggestive lyrics, the single sold over a million copies, and Charles was suddenly being booked at major concert halls, including Carnegie Hall, where he performed for the first time in 1959. The album *The Genius of Ray Charles* was produced the same year and became another best-seller. Around that time the American Broadcasting Corporation (ABC) offered him a very generous contract, including profit sharing and eventual ownership of his master tapes, and between 1953 and 1973 he released 24 albums and 43 singles.

Charles reached a personal milestone in 1965, when, after almost 17 years of addiction, he finally weaned himself from heroin. At the same time, he reached yet another career milestone and began touring the world with an 18-piece band. He found recognition and friendship in countries as far flung as New Zealand, Algeria, Israel, and Japan. He left ABC in 1973, following a dispute with its president, and continued to produce his own recordings. Throughout the 1980's, he continued to tour about nine months a year, playing to large and enthusiastic audiences at home and abroad. He even branched into the field of television commercials, most of which he produced himself. One of these was a Pepsi commercial, *You Got the Right One, Baby, Uh-huh*, that was rated the most memorable commercial of 1991.

Throughout his successes, Charles contributed to many philanthropic causes, including civil rights, African famine relief, and organizations for the hearing impaired. In 1987, he formed the Robinson Foundation for Hearing Disorders with an endowment of a million dollars, and in 1983, he was inducted into the National Association for the Advancement of Coloured People's Hall of Fame. Despite his blindness, he led a very independent life, enjoying television, baseball games and playing cards. He drove a car and repaired tape recorders. He even learned to play chess, which became a passion for him second only to music.

Ray Charles won 11 Grammy Awards. In 1988, he was presented with a Lifetime Achievement Award from the National Academy of Recording Arts and Sciences. He was also inducted into the Rock and Roll Hall of Fame.

For more information on his life, see *Ray Charles* by Sharon Bell Mathis, Crowell, 1973.

Mars Rising, photograph, Phil Davidson

George Eastman 9

"The Father of Kodak"

1854 - 1932

George Eastman, whose name is synonymous with the Kodak camera, was born in July, 1854 in Waterville, New York, the third child and only son of the family. His father operated a commercial college that he had started himself. When George was six, his father died, and from that point on, his childhood was spent in poverty. His mother was forced to take in boarders for income. At the age of 14, he left school and got a full-time job as a messenger in an insurance company, studying French and flute on the side. He soon discovered that he had no musical talent, so he turned his attention to photography, buying almost a hundred dollars' worth of lenses and other equipment. He read everything he could find about photography and even asked a local photographer to teach him even more in his studio. He had a steady job in a bank, but during his spare time, he took pictures at every opportunity.

In those days, outdoor photography required a backpack and a wheelbarrow to haul the equipment.

Eastman wanted to find a way to reduce the bulk and make outdoor photography easier and more enjoyable. One day, he came across an article about a formula for a sensitive gelatin emulsion. The idea excited him so much that he had trouble concentrating on his work as a bank clerk. He experimented with making his own emulsion, sometimes working all night and catching up on his sleep on Saturdays. Finally, he thought he had a good enough process to start a business selling it. He asked an uncle for financial help but was turned down, so he decided to start the business on a part-time basis. He bought the materials, mixed and cooked them in his mother's kitchen, and prepared the emulsion himself. He coated the plates, took his own pictures, developed the negatives, and made his own prints. He also developed a machine for making better photographic plates. During those days, England was the centre of photography, so Eastman quit his job and bought a ticket for London where he obtained a patent for his machine before going back home to continue his business. Soon after, he obtained similar patents in France, Germany, Belgium, and finally, the United States.

All the time he kept testing his emulsion and making improvements. He leased the third floor of a large building in Rochester, New York, and set up his manufacturing business. He was still living with his mother, and she was still taking in boarders. One of the boarders, Colonel Henry Strong, became interested in his work and decided to become a partner. The business got off to a fast start. Eastman hired more workers and began shipping thousands of dry plates to wholesalers. But soon he was getting complaints that the plates were defective. He rushed to a dealer in New York City who had thousands of his plates in stock. After carefully testing them, he discovered that, with time, the plates were indeed losing their sensitivity to light. He recalled all unsold plates, closed the factory and experimented for weeks. Night after night he lay awake, until finally, he traced the root of the problem to a supply of gelatin that he had received. From then on, he tested every supply before accepting it.

His business picked up again, and he turned his attention to cameras, which were still very bulky, with heavy and fragile glass plates. He experimented tirelessly with different kinds of paper to replace the glass and after months and months, he came up with a continuous strip of film. In March 1884, when he was just 30 years old, he applied for a patent for his film and went right back to designing a mechanism for holding the film in the camera. He also moved his operation to a four-storey building in Rochester and formed a corporation of 14 shareholders, the Eastman Dry Plate and Film Company. Henry Strong became the first president, Eastman its treasurer. They opened a sales office in London. When he got too busy to spend enough time on his experiments, he hired a full-time research scientist. Eastman was the first person to create such a position. By June 1888, his company had invented a camera that anyone could use. All it needed was a name. For some reason the letter K appealed to him, and he wanted to use that letter at the beginning and end of the name. He came up with "Kodak." It was so simple that anybody could remember it and it was not a word in any language. To popularize his invention, he also came up with an advertising slogan; "You press the button. We do the rest". The one remaining problem with the invention was that the film was difficult to load, so difficult that one had to buy the camera, shoot the film, and then return the camera to the store for printing and reloading.

By 1889, Eastman succeeded in making a transparent film. When Thomas Edison discovered the Kodak film, he was so impressed that he ordered a big supply. Eastman and Edison became good friends, exchanging ideas for their own inventions. After a great deal of joint research, Thomas Edison invented the movie camera, and in 1900, Eastman came up with the first Kodak Brownie, a camera which sold for a dollar and used a 15-cent roll of film. He had in mind mass production of equipment that the general public could use easily.

Eastman made a fortune, but he never changed his lifestyle. He shared his profits with his employees and donated, anonymously, $20 million to the Massachusetts Institute of Technology. He also donated money to establish free dental clinics for children in Rochester, London, Paris, Rome, Brussels, and Stockholm. He planned a school of music, a theatre and a symphony orchestra for Rochester, and helped fund a medical school and hospital for the University of Rochester. Throughout his successes, he remained simple at heart and shy with strangers, disliking attention and recognition. Ironically, there are very few pictures of him.

He never married, continuing to live with his mother as long as she was alive. In his later years, he suffered from arthritis, and one day in 1932, at the age of 78, he shot himself.

For more information on his life, see *George Eastman and the Early Photographers,* by Brian Coe, Priority Press, 1973.

The Professor, acrylic on masonite, Katherine Fraser

Timothy Eaton 10

"Revolutionary Retailer"

1834 - 1907

The founder of the Eaton's department store empire was born in 1834 in Northern Ireland, the youngest of nine children. His father died two months before his birth, and his mother struggled to raise her children, somehow saving enough money to put a deposit down for Timothy's four-year apprenticeship with one of the best dry-goods merchants in town. The merchant accepted the 13 year-old Timothy on the condition that if he quit at any time before the end of the four-year term, his mother would lose her deposit.

Timothy worked sincerely and enthusiastically, but was always disappointed that no matter how good a job he did, his master did not compliment him or for that matter, even smile. He had to work for 13 hours every day during the week and 19 hours on Saturdays, an 84-hour week. Because his job was thankless and harsh, he often thought of quitting and forfeiting the deposit. His mother told him that she would not force him to endure the torture even though money

was very scarce. Nevertheless, Timothy managed to complete the full term.

By that time, driven by Ireland's potato famine, two of his brothers had already immigrated to Canada and had been asking Timothy to join them. So, in 1851, at the age of 17, he took his deposit money and left his home to try his luck in a new land.

For about 10 years, he worked in country stores near London, Ontario, finally entering a partnership with his brother James in a dry-goods and millinery store in the town of St. Mary's. For eight years he worked relentlessly to build up the business, and in 1869, at the age of 35, decided to go into business for himself. He chose Toronto, where he bought a small business at the corner of Yonge and Queen streets. At the time, there were over 2,000 general stores in Ontario alone, which translated roughly into one store for every hundred inhabitants. Many of the merchants were very well established and were located in busy districts, but because of his limited financial means,

Eaton had to choose a cheaper location. As well, there were two stores within one block of his which, at that time, meant stiff competition.

During those days, merchants priced their goods high, allowing customers to bargain their way to a better deal. The stores were open 12 hours a day or more, and most transactions involved exchanging goods, which often left merchants with goods they could not use. Eaton felt that those practices were not fair either to the merchants or to the customers, and was determined to reform the system. He placed an advertisement " offering goods for cash only and at one price". A few months later, he added another term, this being that " if his goods were not satisfactory, his customers could get their money back". His approach created a sensation. Every merchant was convinced that, with those policies, Eaton could not stay in business long. But he was determined to fight the old system and bought the best quality items, offering them to his customers at as low a price as he could afford. Gradually, he started earning a reputation for selling quality goods at the lowest price.

Employees also benefited from Eaton's innovative approach to store management. He treated them as members of his family, giving them paid sick leave, providing recreation, and otherwise taking care of their welfare. But he did not stop there. He also decided to cut down the hours of operation and announced that his store would close at 6 p.m. every weekday evening and at 1 p.m. on Saturdays, arguing that his employees had the right to enjoy the weekend. Every merchant believed that reducing hours so drastically would cost Eaton a significant share of the market, but he achieved exactly the opposite. Knowing that Timothy Eaton's store would close earlier, most customers went there first and enticed by his

money-back guarantee, made all their purchases right there. Eaton also recognized the value of advertising. He wrote his first advertisements himself in simple, direct language that promised his customers a "square deal." He never let them down. Within five years, 40,000 handbills were being circulated each month to selected customers.

Eaton's stores were the first to have electricity and an elevator. The elevator was such a novelty that, when it was first installed, customers were afraid of getting stuck between floors. For several weeks, the elevator ran with no passengers, save a dummy going continuously up and down. It eventually became so popular that the store had to limit its use to passengers going up. Those going down had to reluctantly take the stairs and, at the time, there were only two floors in the store!

With all these advantages, Eaton's business increased to the point that he was able to open branches in other cities in Canada. Within 25 years of the first store's opening, Eaton's was being called Canada's greatest store.

Timothy Eaton could be described as clean living even by the standards of his time. He was a devout churchgoer, often spending as much time in church as in his business. He believed in helping others, in doing good turns, yet he was also strict. He considered playing cards to be a waste of time and he detested tobacco. He never allowed tobacco goods to be sold in his stores, and in some stores, even playing cards were not sold. Eaton was also an abstainer, a definite social obstacle in Toronto, where an average man, at that time, consumed about 20 ounces of alcohol every day. Not one to give in to peer pressure, Eaton's favourite drink was buttermilk with salt.

He often said that he was thankful for the harsh

treatment he had received during his apprenticeship, because had built a very strong personality in him. He not only learned more about business, but also experienced the value of hard work and learned to be unafraid of trying something different. He believed that sincere service would eventually be rewarded. Moreover, because of his personal experience with harsh treatment, he resolved to treat his own workers better, and he chose them very carefully.

Timothy Eaton died in 1907, at the age of 73.

For more information on his life, see *The Store that Timothy Built*, by William Stephenson, McClelland and Stewart Ltd., Toronto (1969); or *Timothy Eaton and the Rise of the Department Store*, by Joy L. Santiuk, University of Toronto Press, Toronto, 1990.

Deja Vu, watercolour, Bill Miller

Milton Erickson 11

"Tamer of Incredible Physical Handicaps"

1902 - 1980

Milton Erickson's rise to prominence as America's most renowned hypnotherapist likely would not have come about but for the severe handicaps he was forced to live with in his early life. He learned to use his mind in unique ways to force his body to do what doctors had said was impossible.

Erickson was born in 1902, the son of a poor, uneducated farmer. Even when he was a small child it was evident that he was colour-blind, tone-deaf, and dyslexic. At the age of six, he could not differentiate between the number 3 and the letter "m." He went through most of his schooling without realizing the alphabetical arrangement of words in a dictionary. At the age of 17, he had a bout of polio, and as he lay in his bed, he heard the family doctor tell his mother that he would be dead by morning. Wishing to see one more sunset, he begged his mother to move a dresser that was obstructing his view through the window. As the sun set that evening, Erickson slipped into a coma and remained unconscious for the next three days.

Milton did not die, but was left severely paralysed. Although he could see, hear very acutely, and move his eyes, he could speak only with great difficulty and could not move his body. As he lay endlessly in bed, he learned to play mental games. He started studying every sound he heard and learned to recognize who was coming and in what frame of mind they were in, just by the sound of the barn door closing, and how long it took the footsteps to reach the house.

He had been paralysed for about a year when, one day, his mother tied him in a rocking chair as she went about her farm chores and then completely forgot about him. The boy suddenly found himself totally helpless. Soon, however, he noticed that his rocking chair was oscillating slightly and concluded that his thinking about rocking must have caused the chair to rock. He then stared at his hand and tried to recall how he had once used it to hold a pitchfork. For hours he stared until, bit by bit, his fingers began to twitch and move in tiny, uncoordinated ways. He continued to concentrate until the movements became more defined and he could consciously control them. That day was the beginning of his journey to recovery and later self-sufficiency.

He learned that if he could think about walking and fatigue and relaxation, he could get some relief from his pain. He also learned that he could use his imagination to achieve the same effects as an actual physical effort. He recalled how food tasted, how he had once climbed a tree and jumped like a monkey, how his body had made the different twists and turns of normal movement when he was healthy. Fortunately, at that time his youngest sister was learning to walk, and he watched her all day and mentally tried to copy her.

Within a year of his self-rehabilitation program, Erickson was able to walk with crutches. He then enrolled in medicine at the University of Wisconsin, where he was a slow student but received everyone's sympathy and help. A campus physician suggested that he spend the summer outdoors to allow nature to heal his body and mind, so Erickson decided to go on a canoe trip. A friend who had agreed to accompany him backed out at the last minute, but rather than postpone the trip, Erickson set out alone on crutches with two weeks' worth of supplies and $4 in his pocket. He planned to go downstream for a few days, rest and regain his strength, and then return upstream. Often he got stuck, but nearby campers would rescue him. He shared his funny stories with them and they became his friends. He even did some light work for others to earn money to buy more supplies. When it was time to paddle upstream and return home, Erickson had gained enough strength to fight the current. He no longer needed the crutches. The total trip took 10 weeks during which he covered

1,200 river miles. When he arrived home, he had $8 in his pocket and was a robust boy with a good deal of self-confidence. He never used crutches again, although he limped a little and remained prone to periods of vertigo, disorientation, and severe debility.

At the age of 23, while still a medical student, he married his first wife. They had three children, but the marriage ended in divorce 10 years later. He later married his second wife, Elizabeth, and they had five children. When he was 26, Milton Erickson graduated from the University of Wisconsin with both a Masters and Medical Doctor degree. He practiced medicine, but because of his early experience, became interested in hypnosis and so pursued this field, resulting in his becoming a national authority on hypnotherapy. Between 1940 and 1955, he served as the associate editor of the journal *Diseases of the Nervous System*. Then, at 51, polio struck him once more. This time he used self-hypnosis to aid his recovery, and it proceeded much more quickly than during his first experience with the disease. Nevertheless, his leg muscles were giving up on him, and he became mostly confined to wheelchairs.

As soon as he had recovered from the second bout of polio, he found himself with enough extroverted energy to begin the most colourful and rewarding period of his career - as a friend, therapist, teacher, consultant, and eventually national and world leader in clinical hypnosis. In 1957, he founded the American Society of Clinical Hypnosis and served as its president for its first two years, and in 1958 he initiated the *American Journal of Clinical Hypnosis*, which he edited until 1968. By this time, he was recognized as America's top hypnotherapist, and doctors referred their most difficult cases to him. He published hundreds of papers in scholarly journals. His papers and case studies, compiled in a book, are considered to be the standard text on hypnotherapy. In July 1977, a special issue of the *American Journal of Clinical Hypnosis* was published to commemorate his 75th birthday. That same year, he was awarded the Ben Franklin Gold Medal for his outstanding work in hypnotherapy.

The 17 year-old boy, whom a doctor had given a day to live, died in 1980 after an illustrious career. He was 78.

For more information on his life, see *Healing in Hypnosis* by Milton H. Erickson, Irvington Publishers, New York, 1983.

Climbing the Rocks, watercolour, Molly MacIsaac

Sanford Fleming 12

"Builder the Nation's Railroads"

1827-1915

Canada's first postage stamp, one of its national railroads, the world's time zones, and a telegraph cable across the Pacific Ocean all have one phenomenon in common - Sanford Fleming.

Sanford Fleming was born in 1827 in Kirkcaldy, Scotland, where his father ran a sawmill and a construction company. As a student, he had a knack for mathematics and drawing and began learning the fundamentals of surveying, engineering and railroad construction from the early age of 14, when he apprenticed with a prominent local engineer and surveyor. In 1845, at the age of 18, he decided to take his new skills to Canada and join his brother David. After a week at sea, the weather turned so foul that he thought he would not survive, so he wrote a farewell letter to his father, sealed it in a bottle, and tossed it into the sea. Amazingly, seven months later the bottle, with the letter still inside, washed ashore on the Devon coast, where a fisherman found it and delivered it to his father.

The ship survived the storm, and six weeks later it arrived at Quebec City. Fleming continued on to Peterborough, Ontario, then a town of 2,000 people. Here he presented a letter of introduction to Casimir Gzowski, a noted engineer, but Gzowski told him he would find better opportunities in Scotland. Fleming refused to be discouraged and found some work building canal locks and bridges. He also made a detailed survey of Peterborough and engraved and printed its map himself. It was a local hit. Encouraged by the demand for it, Fleming made two more maps, one of Newcastle District, and the other, Cobourg. He also drew a sketch of Toronto Cathedral. With this early experience in Canada under his belt, he moved to Montreal and obtained a license as a surveyor. In June 1849, he and some friends established the Canadian Institute as well as a regular periodical, *The Canadian Journal*. Just a few years earlier, postage stamps had been introduced in Britain and the United States, and Fleming thought Canada should have them too. He designed several different stamps, but it was his "Three-penny Beaver" that became Canada's first postage stamp, issued on April 23, 1851. Always willing to try new adventures, he then took the position of assistant engineer to survey the route for a railway line between Barrie and Georgian Bay. On this job, he endured flies, heat, and rugged landscape. On one occasion, he chased a bear away with his umbrella.

In 1855, he married Jeanie Hall, whom he had met in Peterborough, and together they had four children. By now, he was captivated by the idea of a railway linking Canada's two coasts, so in 1863, he journeyed to England with a petition to build it. He was promised that steps would be taken to release the North-West Territories from the control of the Hudson's Bay Company. Shortly after his return, he was asked to do a survey for a railway linking the eastern provinces. He submitted 15 possible routes and recommended the best choice, based on trading patterns and the value of the adjacent land for cultivation and settlement. He also took part in the railway's actual construction. One of the obstacles here was choosing material for the railway bridges. The commissioner in charge favoured the cheap wooden bridges, while Fleming recommended fireproof iron, finally offering to pay half the cost of the bridges himself. He didn't have to do this, though. By chance, a wooden bridge caught fire from an engine spark, and the Canadian government was convinced of the benefits of iron. Nine years later, the railway was completed, including its iron bridges, and the first train from Halifax reached Quebec City on July 6, 1876.

In 1871, British Columbia joined Confederation on the condition that a railway line connecting her with eastern Canada would be built within a decade.

Prime Minister Sir John A. Mac Donald immediately asked Fleming to do the necessary survey, which required 21 survey crews. In July 1872, accompanied by his son Frank and two friends, he set out from Toronto to review every mile of the proposed route. Hiking through the Yellowhead pass in the Rocky Mountains and then to the west coast, the party finally reached Victoria in 103 days. In spite of his dedication, however, Fleming lost the contract for the railroad's construction, and feeling dejected, left for England in 1876 for a vacation. There, he missed a train because of confusion over its departure time. It occurred to him from this small misfortune that there should be some universal way of describing time, and he came up with the idea of dividing the world into 24 time zones. He published his proposal in the 1879 *Proceedings* of the Canadian Institute. Canada's Governor General read the article and circulated copies to governments throughout the world. As a result, an International Time Conference was held in Rome in 1882 and another in Washington, DC., in October 1884. On January 1, 1885, Universal Standard Time was accepted by most nations.

Even though he had dissociated himself from Canada's national railroad project, he was not left in peace. In March 1880, the House of Commons in Ottawa charged him with "neglect of duties, financial mismanagement and an ill-judged decision on the bridge crossing of the Red River." A royal commission that was set up to examine the charges, accused him of "needless delay in carrying out his duties, of making an unnecessary survey of Grander Inlet, an inadequate one of the large area of muskeg swamps, and of mismanaging public funds on the purchase of steel rails." All of these charges were later found to be without grounds. Fleming had actually been a scapegoat for the politically motivated delays and indecisiveness of the federal government. Instead of punishing him, Canadian Pacific Railway executives George Stephen and Cornelius Van Horne asked him to find a more southerly route through the Rockies. Fleming recommended the Rogers Pass. In 1885, he became a member of the Board of Directors of the CPR, and on June 28, 1886, the first train left Montreal, arriving at the Pacific coast 140 hours later.

Fleming's wife died in 1888, and to fill the void left in his life, he busied himself by working on his idea of a Pacific cable for telegraphing messages across the ocean. He wrote to Mac Donald, who liked the idea very much. After a lot of politicking, Fleming got to work bringing the project to fruition, and on October 31, 1902, the first message was sent over the Pacific cable - a greeting from King Edward VII to the people of Fiji. The first message received in Canada was a congratulatory note from the New Zealand Prime Minister to Sanford Fleming.

From 1880 until his death in 1915, Sanford Fleming also served as the Chancellor of Queen's University in Kingston, Ontario.

For more information on his life, see *Sanford Fleming*, by Lorne Edmond Green, Fitzherny & Whiteside Ltd., 1980.

Country Road, watercolour, Adeline Rockett

Terry Fox 13

"An Extraordinary Fund-Raiser"

1958 - 1981

Although he lived not quite 23 years, Terry Fox became a symbol of courage for all Canadians and a beacon of hope for cancer patients around the world.

Terrance Stanley Fox was born on July 28, 1958, in Winnipeg, the second of four children. His father worked in Winnipeg as a switchman for the Canadian National Railways before moving his family to Vancouver in 1966, to get away from the Manitoba cold.

Terry was an average student. In stature, he was small, and when he sat in the classroom in his usual spot, about three-quarters of the way back, his feet did not touch the floor. But he was athletic, and his grade 8 physical education teacher, Bob McGill, coaxed him into becoming more involved in sports. Under his influence, Terry learned to love basketball and began to aspire to become a physical education teacher. He also started training for cross-country running. He went to the post-game parties following basketball games, but his idea of a good time was really a night playing basketball. He was very disci-

plined and never missed a practice or training session. In grade 11, he played as a starting guard for his high school basketball team, and in grade 12, he shared his school's 'Athlete of the Year Award' with his friend, Doug Alward.

After graduating from high school, Terry enrolled at Simon Fraser University to study kineseology. In November of 1976, he was involved in a car accident but walked away without any serious injuries, except that his right knee became a little sore. A month later, he was still experiencing some pain in that knee, but thinking that it was related to the accident and afraid that he might not be allowed to play basketball, he did not tell anyone. One day in March of 1977, he limped back home from his regular jogging session and went to see a doctor about it. After a series of tests, he was diagnosed as having osteogenic sarcoma, a cancer of the bone, and on March 9, 1977, his right leg was amputated six inches above the knee. He was only 18 years and 8 months old.

The night before his surgery, one of his coaches gave Fox a copy of *Runners' World* which featured a story about Dick Traum, an amputee, who had run in the New York Marathon. That story inflamed Terry's imagination. He realized that losing a leg was not the end of the world, and decided to accept his fate and fight his adversity. That night, he resolved to run across Canada. Within three weeks of the amputation, he wore his first artificial limb, and in another three weeks, he was playing pitch-and-putt golf. Bit by bit, he improved his skill at golf and was soon playing 27 holes a day.

For the next 14 months, Fox received treatments every three weeks at the British Columbia Cancer Control Agency. He suffered the usual side effects of nausea and hair loss, but neither the amputation nor the cancer treatment prevented him from playing basketball. A few months after his surgery, he received a call from Rick Hansen, a wheelchair athlete, who would one day earn fame for his own feats. Hansen invited him to join the Vancouver Cablecars basketball team. Fox agreed and within two months of joining, he was chosen for the national wheelchair basketball games to be held in Edmonton. The Cablecars won the national championship. Fox eventually played on three championship teams. By the 1979-80 season, the Cablecars were rated sixth in the North American Wheelchair Basketball Association and Fox had been chosen as one of the guards for the all-star team.

While in Edmonton, Fox underwent chemotherapy. His doctors predicted that he did not have long to live. He knew his condition but did not want any sympathy or special treatment. Instead, he continued to challenge himself, and in addition to training for wheelchair basketball, he started practicing running. He also got involved in a wheelchair volleyball team under the tutelage of Rika Noda. In January 1979, he started a diary to record his training accomplishments. Until that time, only his friend, Doug Alward, knew about his dream to run across Canada. Now, he told Rika. Initially, he thought it would take him two years to train but he became impatient and decided to speed up his program. He started running 10 miles every day and entered his first race in Prince George, British Columbia, where he finished eighth.

Eventually, he had to tell other people about his dream, particularly his parents. His mother reacted with disbelief, but his father simply asked, "When?". He shared his plans with Blair Mackenzie, the executive director of the British Columbia and Yukon division of the Canadian Cancer Society, telling him that he wanted to raise a million dollars for cancer research. Mackenzie felt that would be impossible, but he agreed to help plan the run.

With Rika Noda, Doug Alward, and Blair Mackenzie, Fox got busy planning his cross-country marathon. The group wrote letters to prospective sponsors, including Ford, who agreed to supply a camper van, and Adidas, who promised running shoes for both Terry and Doug. Other corporations also chipped in, including Imperial Oil, Canada Safeway, Pacific Western Airlines, and Labatt's. While they organized, Fox trained. It was rigorous and difficult. On Christmas Eve of 1979, when he had gone only half a mile, the lower part of his artificial leg broke, and he fell on the sidewalk. He gathered his dignity, picked up the pieces, and hitchhiked home.

On April 12, 1980, Terry Fox started his Marathon of Hope across Canada. He had a good start and fairly good success at fund-raising through the Atlantic provinces but ran into many frustrations in Quebec. Several times, he was almost blown over by the gusts of wind created by passing vehicles, and on one hundred-mile stretch, he collected only $35. At one point, the provincial police asked him to stop the run because it was unsafe. In Ontario, however, he was received very warmly and welcome signs awaited him in almost every town. A police patrol escorted him from one end of the province to the other. He was so successful that special requests for his appearance in this or that town added more miles to his total journey.

He never completed his run through Ontario. By the end of August, when he was just a few miles from Thunder Bay, he had to stop because he was unable to breathe normally. By that time, he had run 3,339 miles and raised $1.7 million, almost doubling his original goal of $1 million. He went to Winnipeg for treatment and then flew home to Vancouver. His cancer had spread to his lung.

While he fought for his life, Canadians prayed for his recovery. They also helped him reach a new personal goal to collect a dollar for each Canadian, or a total of $22 million. The Canadian Television Network sponsored a four-hour telethon on September 9, 1980, and raised a total of $10.5 million. For the next several weeks, donations poured in.

Terry Fox died on June 28, 1981, just one month shy of his 23rd birthday. Since 1980, the Terry Fox Run, held each September, has become an annual Canadian fund-raising event for cancer research, and in 1983, Fox was listed in *The Guinness Book of World Records* for raising $24.7 million in 143 days.

For more information on his life, see *Terry Fox: His Story*, by Leslie Scrivener, McClelland and Stewart Ltd., 1983.

Montreal le soir, acrylic on canvas, Andrea House

Buckminster Fuller 14

"Designer of Geodesic Domes"

1895-1983

Did being cross-eyed for the first four years of his life have something to do with Richard Buckminster Fuller's later success as one of America's most innovative and imaginative architectural designers? No one will ever know, but there is no question about the impact Fuller has had on the world of design.

Fuller was born on July 12, 1895, near Boston. As a child, he showed an exceptionally inquisitive mind, which created many problems for him, although he managed to adapt and make his way through primary and secondary school. His father died when Fuller was 13, leaving the family very poor. Still, Fuller was able to follow a five-generation family tradition and enroll in Harvard. Unfortunately, this was hardly the place for an unconventional person, and his unusual ideas and overly enthusiastic personality, caused classmates to avoid him. Lonely and depressed, he neglected his studies and later blew his money on a wild party expedition to New York City and was expelled before completing the year. His family then punished him by sending him to Quebec to work as a machinist in a cotton mill. A year later, he was accepted back at Harvard, but once again was asked to leave.

When World War I broke out, he served in the Navy, commanding a family-owned boat that hunted German submarines and later rescued pilots whose planes had crashed. In 1917, he married Anne Hewlett, and a year and a half later, they had a baby girl. She was always ill, and despite their loving care and the best medical treatment of the time, she died before turning four years old. Fuller was devastated. He loved his daughter dearly and felt especially guilty because, at the time of her death, he had been at a football game. For the rest of his life, he could not think of her without being choked with emotion.

Somehow, Fuller managed to carry on, accepting his father-in-law's offer to be president of his own brick making company. The family moved to Chicago, where Fuller instituted several improvements in brick making. During this period, he also fathered his second child. In 1927, his father-in-law also died, and internal corporate problems, coupled with government regulations and union demands, forced the closure of the company. That proved to be the lowest point of his life and he considered himself a complete failure. He had failed in college. He had failed in business. He had no means of supporting his family and no money for any of his projects. The harder he tried, the more he seemed to fail.

One night, as he wandered along the shores of Lake Michigan, fully intending to drown himself, he suddenly realized that as an integral part of the universe he had no right to take his own life. That thought did not lift him out of his depression, but it did provide him with enough energy to get through two more decades of frustration and ridicule. He developed the belief that he was working for no one but the universe. He was determined to hunt for ways of making more with less and to work for the well-being of people everywhere. He also believed that much of his pain had arisen from selfish acts when he had placed his own needs over those of others and when he had approached life with the attitude, "What's in it for me?".

As a result, he resolved to commit his life to benefiting others, but did not have a clear idea of how to do that. For the next two years, he did nothing but think, while his family scraped by, living in a Chicago slum. He refused to speak, for fear, that the speech patterns he had learned over the years would get in the way of thought. Accounting to no one, he freed his mind so that it could explore and wrestle with all the questions that came to it. Eventually, using his knowledge of tools, metals, machines, and technology, he started thinking of constructive designs, and within a

short time, he turned into a prolific designer. Unfortunately, his designs and ideas went largely unnoticed.

He coined the name Dymaxion - dynamic plus maximum plus ion. He designed a Dymaxion house and a Dymaxion car, the latter of which was on the road in 1933. Unfortunately, the car was involved in a fatal accident, and even though Fuller was not at fault, the car came under fire in the press and was thus doomed.

For the next 10 years, Fuller used all his skills and imagination to design many things, always with the idea of getting more for less. He did not achieve any significant success. Between 1944 and 1945, he produced two prototype Dymaxion houses, but they were never popular. At some point, the idea of geodesics came to his fertile mind, and he slowly developed the idea of dome-shaped structures that could be both lighter and stronger than other styles of architecture. He felt that they could be manufactured in mass quantities in a factory and assembled easily on site. Although he tried several models, continually demonstrating them to the public, for several years no one paid much attention to the idea.

His big break came in 1952, when the Ford Motor Company was celebrating its 50th anniversary. Henry Ford II remembered that his grandfather had dreamed of building a dome over the courtyard at their Dearborn, Michigan plant, but the experts advised him that the lightest dome would weigh 160 tons which was far more than any foundation could bear. Someone mentioned Fuller's dome and Fuller guaranteed Ford a dome that would weigh only eight and a half tons. He was given permission to go ahead. Despite having no experience in a large-scale project like the one Ford planned, Fuller completed his dome on schedule. The effect was better than Ford could have imagined, and Fuller's ideas were suddenly in demand.

On June 29, 1954, Buckminster Fuller was awarded a patent for his dome design. The U.S. Department of Defense then asked him to design domes for polar conditions, while the U.S. Marines wanted them for temporary shelters. In 1957, a dome was chosen to house a concert hall in Hawaii. The materials were flown in, and in less than 24 hours after they were unpacked, the building was filled with 1,800 people. It provided the best acoustics that the music director had ever experienced.

Domes began to pop up in all sizes for widely different purposes. The hottest demand came from fairs around the world. American exhibitors recognized the geodesic dome as a uniquely American contribution to architecture. By the late 1950's, Fuller's domes were appearing all over the world - and appearing quickly. At the 1956 Kabul Trade Fair, a dome 135 feet across and 100 feet high was built within two days.

A dome Fuller designed for the 10th International Design Fair in Milan, Italy, won the Grand Prize. Its skin was composed entirely of paper. Later, a dome 200 feet in diameter captured most of the attention at the 1959 Moscow World Fair. By that time, more than a hundred companies were licensed to build geodesic domes, and by 1966, there were over 5,000 such structures in 50 countries. Just six years later, there were more than 50,000 domes in existence. Fuller's masterpiece was the United States Pavilion at Expo '67 in Montreal. It was 200 feet high and 250 feet across.

In June 1954, North Carolina State College conferred on him an honorary degree of Doctor of Design. Although Fuller never did graduate from college, he received over 40 honorary degrees, including one from Oxford in England. Fuller died on July 1, 1983.

For more information on the life of Buckminster Fuller, see *Buckminster Fuller* by Robert McHale, 1962.

Johnson Lake-Looking West, Banff, acrylic on canvas, Elaine Tweedy

Charles Goodyear 15

"The India Rubber Man"

1800 - 1850

Charles Goodyear was the inventor of a process that made rubber one of the world's most useful and versatile natural resources.

He was born on December 19,1800, in New Haven, Connecticut, the son of a farm implements manufacturer. As a child he wanted to be a minister, but his father could not afford to send him to school. When he turned 17, he was apprenticed to a hardware dealer in Philadelphia until he was 21, at which point he entered into partnership with his father. Three years later, he married Clarissa Beecher, the daughter of an innkeeper, and eventually opened his own store, also in Philadelphia. But he gave lines of credit to his customers too easily and then couldn't collect on them, so by the depression of 1830, he was broke and had to close down.

Before long, his family was going hungry. Unable to find a job in Philadelphia, he travelled to New York City, where he happened to see some rubber clothing in the shop window of the Roxbury India Rubber Company. He had read about rubber and its usefulness but had never seen any clothing made from it. He asked the store's owner if he could inflate the life preserver and immediately discovered a fault in the valve. He offered to make a better one.

Although his children needed food, he bought the life preserver, returned to Philadelphia and designed a better valve. He went back to New York City and tried to show his valve to the store owner but the owner was not interested. The store owner was facing another, more serious problem. The hot weather had turned most of his rubber goods into a soft, sticky mess. He asked Goodyear if he knew anyone who could find a way to keep rubber goods from melting in summer and turning brittle in winter. Then and there, Goodyear determined that he would discover the necessary process. Although he knew little about the chemistry of rubber, he was confident that he could learn by trial and error, so he bought some cheap rubber gum and set up a makeshift laboratory in the kitchen of his home. He then melted some rubber, added turpentine, and rolled the concoction out on his wife's breadboard.

In the meantime, Goodyear's many creditors got tired of waiting and had him thrown into prison where he fell ill. Still, he kept thinking about the rubber problem. His wife sold some of her wedding linen to buy food and then spent part of her hard-earned money on raw rubber and chemicals so that her husband could experiment while in prison. The jailer was sympathetic and let him work at a table and stove. His rubber experiments did not pay off immediately, but while still in prison, Goodyear invented a new farm tool which earned him enough money to pay some of his debts. As a result, he was released.

With further financial assistance from a boyhood friend, he was able to continue his experiments for about a year, after which he borrowed more money, left his family in Connecticut, and went to New York City to do further research. Other friends gave him the necessary work space and chemicals to experiment with raw rubber, magnesium, and quicklime, from which he was able to produce a smooth, non-sticky rubber. He brought his family to Staten Island where they helped him make more rubber goods so that he could open a store on Broadway. Just when he appeared to be on his way to entrepreneurial success, he discovered that his rubber could be ruined by common household acids such as vinegar and apple juice. Once more he was in debt, but his wife encouraged him to keep trying.

He formed a partnership with Nathaniel Haywood, who had patented a process for mixing sulphur and rubber. Together, they produced a good rubber coating and Goodyear obtained the patent for the process in 1839. He showed his product to the U.S. Post Office and received an order for 150 mail-bags. Once again, his family helped him make the goods, but once again, they proved to be flawed. In hot weather, the heavy bags became soft and pulled away from their handles. People then lost confidence in his rubber. Many called him the rubber lunatic, and again and again, he found himself in prison for debt. Friends advised him to find a regular job to support his family.

But he refused to give up. He kept experimenting with different chemicals and processes, until one day, he accidentally dropped a lump of rubber on the hot stove. When he picked it up, he discovered that it had been charred on the outside but was pliable and smooth on the inside. He immediately recognized that a combination of sulphur and heat was the magic formula that would solve the problem. He continued experimenting with different temperatures and levels of sulphur content and eventually formulated the process that he called vulcanizing, after the name of the fire god, Vulcan. He finally obtained a patent for his process in 1844.

Borrowing still more money, this time from his brother-in-law, he built a large brick oven and continued to refine the rubber-making process. He then took his family to Europe and discovered that in England, one, Thomas Hancock, had stolen his idea and secured the English patent. Although he launched an expensive lawsuit and lost, he was able to sell some English rights to manufacturers and later wrote a book called *Gum Elastic and Its Varieties*. He also entered a $30,000 rubber display in the International Exhibition in London.

While living in England, both he and his wife were often ill, and his wife died in March 1853. After a year of loneliness, he married a 20 year-old woman from London, and they moved to France. There, he entered his goods in another large display. He then secured patents in several European countries and sold rubber rights to manufacturers in France and Germany. But the two expensive exhibitions had pushed him into debt again, and now he found himself in prison in France. Sixteen days later, his son arranged for his release and it was not long afterward that Napoleon III awarded him the Grand Medal of Honour for his rubber invention.

After eight years abroad, he returned to the United States and bought a fine home in Washington, D.C. But the years of poverty and strain had broken his health. One day he heard that his daughter Cynthia was dying in Connecticut, and on his way to see her, he became ill in New York City and died in a hotel there on July 1, 1850.

For more information on his life, see *India Rubber Man: The Story of Charles Goodyear* by Ralph Frank Wolf, or *Oh, What an Awful Mess! The Story of Charles Goodyear*, by Robert M. Quackenbush, Englewood Cliffs, N.J., 1980.

Above Lake O'hara, watercolour on rice paper, Yuriko Igarashi-Kitamua

Sir Edmund Hillary 16

"The Mount Everest Climber"

Born in 1919

The leader of the first expedition to reach the summit of Mount Everest was born in New Zealand in 1919. Edmund Percival Hillary was the son of a beekeeper. He was a soft-spoken and shy child who was also a bit of a perfectionist. With the help of his mother, who had been a teacher, he finished elementary school two years earlier than normal, and then found himself in high school too young, too small, and very uncomfortable. Nevertheless, he stayed in school and joined the other students in various activities, including a weekend ski trip to Mount Ruapehu when he was 16. Until that time, he had never seen snow. He was instantly mesmerized by the mountains, and from then on, he spent a great deal of his time in New Zealand's Southern Alps.

After completing high school, he attended university for couple of years before leaving, without a degree, to become a full-time beekeeper for half the year and to spend the other half mountain climbing. As a beekeeper, he was exempted from serving in World

War II, but after about a year, he asked his father to release him so that he could join the service. He joined the Air Force and became a navigator. Just before the end of the war, his boat was blown out of the water and he suffered serious burns. Following the war, he went right back to beekeeping and mountain climbing and became an active member of the New Zealand Alpine Club. He eventually climbed most of the peaks in the country.

One day, one of the climbers in his group slipped and fell straight toward him. In a fraction of a second, he looked down and decided that it was safer to let her go by. When she had stopped falling, he climbed down to see how she was. Except for some bruises, she was all right. Her name was Louise, and from that day, Hillary became particularly interested in her.

Hillary and his brother took over their father's beekeeping business in 1950, and in 1951, Edmund toured the Himalayas through the New Zealand Alpine Club. Everyone noticed his exceptional enthusiasm for climbing and excellent skills on ice, and he was therefore quickly invited to join a British team to explore the possibility of climbing Mount Everest. But they would have competition in the race to the top. In 1952, a Swiss expedition, led by a Sherpa guide, Tenzing Norguay, climbed to 28,000, feet before a monsoon forced them to retreat. Soon after the monsoon, the team made a second attempt, but because of the approaching winter, they only got to 26,000 feet.

In 1953, Hillary was again invited to join the British team. Soon after doing so, he became friends with Norguay who had been chosen the senior guide for the expedition. The team left Katmandu early in May 1953 and reached 26,000 feet, where they set up camp. From there, two members explored the area but returned very exhausted. Hillary and Norguay then set out and were able to climb to 27,900 feet, where they camped with the thermometer in their tent registering minus 27 degrees C. The next day, they decided to stay in camp because of very strong winds, but the following day, May 29, the winds had calmed down, and they left camp at six in the morning and reached the summit of Mount Everest at about 11:30 that same morning.

Almost immediately after coming down the mountain, Hillary was knighted. He had hardly returned to New Zealand when he received an invitation to take a lecture tour of England. Since he did not want to be separated from Louise, he married her within a few weeks, and from September to February they traveled in Europe, Canada, and the United States. For the next two years Hillary stayed in New Zealand, looking after the beekeeping business. During that period, he and Louise had a son and a daughter. He was then invited to join an expedition to Ant-arctica to lay depots for Vivian Fuchs, who was attempting to cross Antarctica from west to east, passing through the South Pole. Hillary reached the South Pole on January 4, 1958.

After returning to New Zealand, he gave up on beekeeping for good and he and Louise had another daughter. By now, he was intrigued by new challenges, one of them being an ascent of Mount Everest from the Tibetan side. In 1960, he joined an expedition, this time attempting the climb without carrying oxygen. At 23,000 feet, Hillary suffered from cerebral edema and had to retreat miserably down to base camp. At 27,000 feet, another member collapsed with pulmonary edema, and the whole expedition was abandoned. Hillary stayed in Nepal to build a school. For the next 10 years, his family lived in New Zealand while he spent much of his time in the Himalayas, building a dozen schools, a hospital, a number of bridges and water pipelines, and even an air field at Lukla. He also led an expedition to Antarctica and climbed the super peak of Mount Herschel. His family then decided to spend a year in Nepal, and in January 1975, they moved to Katmandu. Not long afterwards, Hillary's wife and one of their daughters were killed in a plane crash. Hillary had been helping to set up a hospital at the time of the crash and he managed to finish the project. Once it was completed, he no longer knew what to do with his life.

With the help of some friends, he produced a two-hour film on mountaineering, but it was never profitable. Then he decided to explore the entire length of the river Ganges in India, and with the cooperation of the Indian government, he started the trip in August 1977. Although the expedition itself was successful in reaching the river's headwaters, Hillary once again suffered cerebral edema and had to be carried down and rushed to hospital. After a few days, he returned to Nepal to work on other projects, including raising money to run his new hospital.

In 1981, at the age of 62, Sir Edmund Hillary was invited to lead an American expedition to Mount Everest from Tibet. He was delighted to discover that Tenzing Norguay was also on the team. Although older than Hillary, Norguay was in much better physical condition. In spite of the quality of the team's leadership, there were many frustrations and disappointments, including bad weather, poor food, inadequate equipment, and too many people. Hillary himself continued to experience headaches and breathing problems at high altitudes, and after reaching 21,500 feet, the team abandoned its attempt.

In September 1982, Hillary visited India as a tourist, and in 1984 he was appointed New Zealand's High Commissioner to India. After completing the four-year term, he retired to New Zealand.

For more information on his life, see *Two Generations* by Edmund and Peter Hillary, Hodder & Stoughton, Toronto, 1984.

The Window, watercolour, Natasha Manelis

Harry Houdini 17

"Master of Escape"
1874 - 1926

Such was Houdini's fame that the modern English language has virtually appropriated his name: a Houdini is an escape artist of uncanny talent. Houdini was born Ehrich Weiss in 1874 in Budapest, Hungary. The third of five children, his father was a rabbi. Shortly after his birth, the family moved to the United States and settled in Appleton, Wisconsin.

The Weiss family were poor immigrants. Ehrich and his brothers had to earn money shining shoes and selling newspapers. Already as a child, he was an entertaining trickster. When he was nine years old, he hung ropes from a tree branch in his backyard, tied a wooden bar to the ropes and showed off his tricks. Impressed by his performance and interest, one of his friends asked him to be in his five-cent circus, and there, he started practicing rope escapes. One day, his mother noticed that pieces of her cake were disappearing. To prevent him from eating too much, she locked the cake in a kitchen drawer, but no matter where she kept it or which lock she used, the cake continued to disappear. She later discovered that a locksmith had been teaching her son how to open any lock.

When he was 13, his family moved to New York City. There his father fell ill, so to help his family, Ehrich performed tricks as often as he could. At one point, he came home and asked his mother to shake him, and as she shook, coins fell from different parts of his body. For about two years, he worked as an assistant necktie cutter, and during his spare time, practiced magic and learned card and rope tricks. He read books on magic and gave magic shows in local neighbourhoods. When he was 16, he read a book on the life of Jean Eugene Robert-Houdin, the greatest magician of France. He was so impressed by the man's life and work that he decided to try a magician's career himself. Within a few days, he left his job and decided to change his name. Since his friends called him Ehrie, he decided to become Harry, and he took the name Houdini from his French idol.

His younger brother, Theo, was also interested in magic, and together, they promoted themselves as the Houdini Brothers. Using a second-hand magic trunk, they did a simple and rapidly paced show, and their name became well known, not only in the New York area, but elsewhere in the United States as well. The brothers attended the 1893 World's Fair in Chicago and performed their act on an outdoor stage. The next year, they travelled to Coney Island, New York. There he married Wilhelmina Beatrice Rahner, commonly known as Bess, after they had known each other for only 10 days. She was 18 and he was 19. Since Theo was growing too big for the magic trunk, she took over that act.

Harry and Bess started giving six to 20 shows a day in dime museums where people paid a dime to watch a variety of shows. No matter how hard they worked, they didn't earn much money. People were just not very impressed by their tricks. After a year of the dime shows, they joined the Welsh Brothers' Circus for $25 a week, half of which Harry sent to his mother in New York City. Apart from their own shows, Harry and Bess sold trick decks of cards, toothpaste, and soap to the circus goers. From an old Japanese acrobat, he learned how to swallow objects, a technique he later used to hide tools for his escape acts. Around that time, he became very interested in locks, and wherever the circus went, he visited locksmith shops. He studied locks and took them apart to find out how they worked. At night, he read books on locks. Whenever he had money to spare, he bought a pair of handcuffs, until he had a large collection. When the circus season was over, he bought a part interest in a travelling show, and the press took an interest in his acts. Occasionally, he would invite policemen to handcuff him, but no handcuffs could hold him.

Despite all his efforts, the travelling show failed, and Houdini and his wife moved to the midwest, where they worked off and on, here and there. In Kansas, they joined Dr. Hill's Concert Company, performing to attract people to whom Dr. Hill could sell his medicines. To compensate for the slow business during the winter, Dr. Hill held seances and asked Houdini to play the role of the spiritualist. For a while, Houdini became interested in spirits but was soon convinced that the whole thing was a hoax.

Even after seven years of very hard work and thousands of very successful performances, Houdini was neither rich nor famous. To earn money, he wrote a 16-page booklet called *Magic Made Easy*, but very few people bought it. He then approached four newspapers and offered to sell his handcuff secret for $20, but no one showed any interest. Unable to find a steady job, he once again joined the Welsh Brothers' Circus and took on the dime museums, performing as many as 20 shows a day. In one of these shows, Martin Beck, the manager of the largest chain of theatres in the West, was in the audience. Beck told Houdini that he was a rotten showman, trying to do too much and giving a 30 minute act in 10 minutes. Beck then hired him, offering much higher pay than Houdini had ever earned before. Under Beck's guidance, Houdini became a stage star in the west and midwest but still did not have a name in the east. He went to New York City to try making it on his own, but he could not make any headway, so he decided to try London, Paris, and Berlin.

In May 1900, he and Bess left for London. They did not know anyone in Europe, and no one had heard of them, so Houdini visited a theatre manager and showed him some of his newspaper clippings.

The manager agreed to hire him if Houdini could get out of the cuffs at Scotland Yard, a feat he accomplished with ease. The constabulary of Scotland Yard treated his challenge as a joke at first, but Houdini persuaded them to handcuff him and tie him up and give him a time limit in which to free himself. They gave him an hour, but before they even left the room, he was out of his restraints. Astonished, the theatre manager hired him on the spot, and very soon, stories about his unique skills started appearing in several newspapers. Suddenly, Houdini was a famous man in England. He had even greater success in Berlin, where he became Germany's best-known showman. During the next four years, he and Bess traveled all over Europe. Everywhere, the newspapers wrote stories about him and people crowded into theatres to see him. By the time he left Europe for the United States, he was earning $1,200 a week.

Even when his show was polished and professional, he continued to practice every day, setting aside part of each day for exercises to keep his body strong. He built a large bathtub to practice holding his breath for underwater escapes, working up to four minutes and 16 seconds. In winter, he poured ice water into the tub to train himself for a jump into a cold river. In addition to his daily shows, he gave special shows to raise money for hospitals, prisons, old people's homes, and World War I relief.

When he was 39 and had become the best-known magician and escape artist in America, his mother died. To overcome that sorrow, he worked even harder. For a while, he again became interested in spirits and tried to contact his mother, but encountered only frustrations. Then in October 1926, a young man visited his dressing room in Montreal and asked if he could throw a punch at Houdini's stomach.

Houdini accepted the challenge. The man caught him by surprise before he could brace himself for the blow. Nevertheless, he asked the man to try again and hit him, and for the second punch, he tightened his stomach muscles so that his stomach was as hard as a plank. The next day, on his way to a show in Detroit, he ran a high fever. He went ahead and did the show, collapsing immediately afterward. He was rushed to hospital, where doctors removed a ruptured appendix. They were too late. A few days later, on October 31, 1926, at the age of 52, Harry Houdini died.

For more information on his life, see *Houdini: His Life and Art* by James Randi, Grosset & Dunlap, 1976, or *Escape: The Life of Harry Houdini* by Florence Meiman White, J. Messner, New York, 1979.

Ravine View, acrylic on masonite, Herman Goigner

Samuel Gridley Howe 18

"Founder: Perkins Institute for the Blind"

1801 - 1876

The founder of America's first school for the blind, Samuel Gridley Howe, was born on November 10, 1801, near Boston, Massachusetts. He was raised in a community where everyone belonged to one political party while his father belonged to the other, and consequently was constantly teased and sometimes persecuted. Because of his political differences, his father had trouble collecting money for several large government contracts on which he had worked, and his prosperous business was almost ruined. As a result, he could afford to finance the education of only one of his three boys, and since Samuel proved to be the most promising, he was sent to Brown University in Providence, Rhode Island.

Howe graduated from Brown in 1821 and then enrolled in Harvard Medical School, from which he graduated in 1824. With his degree in medicine, he volunteered his services in the Greeks' war of independence against the Turks and served for six years. During this period, he contracted a fever which almost killed him and managed to weaken his constitution for the rest of his life. He returned to Boston in 1831 with a record of romantic adventures in Greece but no medical practice. He had, however, become famous for working on various causes. In 1829, the Massachusetts State Legislature had passed a law to establish a New England asylum for the blind. A few trustees had been appointed and they selected Howe as their director.

Realizing that nothing was being done for blind children anywhere in America, Howe accepted the challenge. He knew nothing about teaching the blind, and there was no one in Boston to instruct him, so as his first step, he journeyed to Europe to study the work that was being done there, especially at the Institute for the Blind in Paris. While in Germany, he got into trouble with the Prussian police because he had helped some Polish refugees in the past. He was jailed for six weeks and forced to pay his own expenses as a prisoner. Many years later, when he had become world-famous, the King of Prussia awarded him a gold medal for his services. Out of curiosity, Howe had the medal appraised and was surprised to find that it was worth exactly the amount he had paid his Prussian jailer for food.

Following his return to Boston from Europe, Howe opened his school for the blind in the house he had inherited from his father. It was 1832 and he had six blind pupils. To experience first-hand the problems a blind person faces, he went about his day blindfolded. He also spent long hours with bits of twine and glue, twisting them into shapes of letters stuck to sheets of cardboard so that the blind children could learn the alphabet by feeling the rough surface with their fingertips. Because of his personal dedication, every child regarded him as a loving father, and he cultivated a spirit of courage and hope. He never let the children feel sorry for themselves. From the very first day, the guiding motto of the institution was, "Obstacles are things to overcome."

But the school suffered financial difficulties from the beginning. In its first six months, all the money was gone, and Howe was faced with a debt of $300. To raise money, he publicized the school's work, on behalf of the blind, and ladies from Boston and cities nearby held fund-raising fairs, while a prominent Bostonian named Perkins offered his big house for the school, on the condition that it raise $50,000 for operating costs. Howe managed to come up with that sum and moved the school to the Perkins mansion, which thereafter, became known as the Perkins Institute.

In 1837, Howe heard of a girl named Laura Bridgman who was living on a farm near Hanover, New Hampshire, and who was not only blind but also deaf and dumb from an attack of scarlet fever. Howe readily obtained her parents' consent to take her to the Perkins Institute, and in time, she became his most famous pupil. He treated her with the devotion of a parent, becoming her personal teacher. Through his efforts, she grew up to become an intelligent, happy, and active woman. Charles Dickens once visited the Perkins Institute and met Laura Bridgman, and she became the subject of an article in his book, *American Notes*. It was through that book that Helen Keller's mother learned about Laura Bridgman and the Perkins Institute and decided to get some help for Helen.

By 1839, when the institute had outgrown even the big Perkins house, Howe bought a large hotel which became home to the school until 1912. He started taking in blind children who also had mental disabilities. At first, they were enrolled in the institute, but Howe decided that it was not wise to mix normal blind children with those with disabilities, so he bought a lot in South Boston and put up a new building for the special needs children. At that time, nobody did anything for such children, but Howe worked hard to make them happy. Although he was faithful to his duties at Perkins, he never missed a day at this second institution, which presented a far greater challenge. Because of his dedication, he became a friend of all the distinguished citizens of New England of that time - writers, statesmen, clergymen, and other leaders.

Howe pioneered the printing of books with raised type, and from 1841-1842, utilizing that method, he published the Bible in eight volumes. The Braille System was not known in America at that time. He also worked for prison reform and aid to discharged convicts, and improved methods of instructing the deaf. He became an active abolitionist (for the abolition of slavery), and his wife Julia Ward Howe, founded and edited the abolitionist journal *Commonwealth* (1851). During the Civil War, he served on the Sanitary Commission and the American Freeman's Inquiry Commission. After the war, he served on a three man committee that recommended the annexation of Santo Domingo (1871). He wrote numerous textbooks for the blind and also published *Historical Sketch of the Greek Revolution* (1828).

He developed his techniques mainly through trial and error. He never hesitated in acknowledging his mistakes and to change whenever he felt it was warranted. He was the first person to demonstrate that it was possible to teach a person who was both deaf and blind. During his days, the Perkins Institute was the outstanding school for the blind, and he, the leading authority. His prestige was so great that his endorsement was often sought for various causes outside of his own specialty.

On the morning of January 4, 1876, he left home as usual to walk to work. He had gone only a few steps when he fell and injured himself. After a few days in bed, he passed away at the age of 74.

For more information on his life, see *A Light in the Dark: the Life of Samuel Gridley Howe* by Milton Meltzer. Published by Thomas Y. Crowell, 1964.

Jasper Winter, watercolour, Barb Brooks

Mother Jones 19

"The Little Lady with Extraordinary Courage"

1830 - 1930

When Mother Jones died after 100 years of life, the American worker lost one of its most staunch and outspoken allies. Travelling to labour trouble spots throughout North America, Mother Jones changed the lives of millions of workers.

Mother Jones was born Mary Harris on May 1, 1830, in Cork, Ireland, the eldest of three children. Her father, like his father before him, was deeply involved in the movement for Irish independence. When Mary was two years old, her grandfather was hanged for his work on behalf of Ireland's sovereignty. Three years later, her father was being hunted down. He managed to escape to the New World where he found work building railroads and canals. For the next six years, Mary's mother worked very hard in Ireland to feed her children, and when Mary was 11, her father was finally able to send for his family.

The four-week long ocean voyage to North America was a nightmare. The passengers had no room to stretch, no fresh air to breathe, no pure water to drink, and not enough food. When the family finally arrived, tired and hungry, they settled in Toronto. There, Harris attended a free public school. She was an excellent student and graduated in 1847, but because she was a woman, was not allowed to attend the teachers' training school and had to be satisfied learning dressmaking from her mother and working out of her own home.

Three years later, when the doors to the teacher's school were finally opened to women, Mary enrolled and at the age of twenty-two, became a qualified teacher. As a Roman Catholic, she was barred from teaching in Toronto. Determined to find a place of her own, she left home and spent some time in Maine as a private tutor. She taught for a year in a convent school in Michigan, before moving to Chicago, where she supported herself as a seamstress. When she was 30, she found a teaching job in Memphis, Tennessee, and moved there, taking a room in a ghetto where many emancipated Irish immigrants lived. Here she met George Jones, an iron worker who became very active in labour unions, and married him. The next few years were happy ones for her. Although the whole country was in turmoil because of the Civil War, Memphis was relatively calm, even when it fell to the Union Army.

George and Mary had four children within seven years and their future looked very promising. In the fall of 1867, following an exceptionally wet spring and a hot, humid summer, yellow fever struck the city of Memphis. Within a month, Mary Jones had lost her husband and all her children. Mary applied for a permit to enter quarantined homes and help other families. She gave baths to feverish and delirious victims, fed those who could not feed themselves, and took care of children whose parents lay dying.

With the onset of frost in November, the epidemic disappeared. Jones packed her few possessions and moved back to Chicago, where she set up a storefront dressmaking shop. Within four years, another tragedy struck when the city was almost totally destroyed by a catastrophic fire that raged for three days leaving more than 300 people dead and 90,000 homeless. In that fire, she lost her shop and all her possessions. She was 41 years old - a widow with no family.

She moved into the basement of a church that served as a temporary shelter and quickly busied herself helping other victims. From that day on, she lived without property and on very little money. Occasionally, she earned some money from union activities, but often she simply depended upon friends to supply whatever necessities she lacked.

The events of her life had made her acutely aware of the indifference of the wealthy to the suffering of the poor. In Memphis, death from yellow fever had been largely confined to poor neighbourhoods. The rich had been able to leave the city and escape the plague. In Chicago, she had seen the vast difference in the lives of the rich and poor. She sewed clothes for wealthy people while her own neighbours were struggling immigrant families. Convinced that something had to be done, she joined the Knights of Labor.

Since women could not become members, she joined as a "supporter" and listed her trade as "dressmaker." She spent more and more time at the hall, listening to splendid speakers. At first, she sat as a silent observer, but slowly began to speak out. She urged the members to bring more workers into the movement. Around the union hall, she became known as a woman with a quick brain and an even quicker tongue. Mary Jones was small, only five feet tall and 100 pounds. She dressed well and spoke well, with a good command of the working-man's way of speaking. She had a low and pleasant voice, and there was an intensity in her speech and a fluidity to her phrases that made audiences listen to and believe in her.

She spent the next two decades travelling to different cities and speaking at union meetings. In the early 1890s, when she was supporting the coal miners' strike in West Virginia and Pennsylvania, the miners began to call her " Mother Jones", as she led the fight against the cruel conditions of the workers. She lived with their families, drank with them in the taverns, and spoke their language. At meetings, she stamped her feet, shouted, gestured, scolded, and shamed them, urging them to join the union, to seek change through collective strength. She shook workers out of their apathy and fear. She gave them energy. She gave them conviction. She could keep the strikers loyal, month after month, on empty stomachs and behind prison bars. She earned that loyalty by suffering the empty stomach and standing behind the prison bars with them, declaring that "to be in prison is no disgrace."

She moved fearlessly in the mining camps. On one occasion, she walked up to a guard who was pointing a gun at her and put her hand over the barrel of the gun. On another, she organized the wives of the miners into a ragtag army. With brooms, mops, and tin washtubs, she marched them to the mine entrance. The terrible din of the washtub band and the unusual appearance of the women so frightened the mules that everyone had to stop working. Mother Jones's army maintained that unusual picket line at the mine entrance until the company capitulated and agreed to meet with the miners to discuss their grievances.

Mother Jones lost more often than she won, but defeat never seemed to dishearten her. She never lost faith in the rightness of the cause or in the ultimate victory of the worker. She often compared the workers' plight to that of the slaves and spoke of the labour movement as a latter-day Civil War. She came to be known as "the miners' angel."

Her concerns were by no means limited to problems of miners. She also fought on behalf of children working in factories. In 1903, she organized the March of the Mill Children from Kensington, Pennsylvania to Sagamore Hill, the summer estate of President Theodore Roosevelt. The 125-mile, 22-day march was covered, in its entirety, by the New York Times, but Roosevelt did not open the gates of his estate to her or her band nor did he carry her fight to Congress.

Defeated but undaunted, she continued her fight against economic injustice. She crisscrossed the continent, participating in strikes, raising funds, and speaking at conferences. She joined union efforts in the copper mines of Michigan, Arizona, and Montana. She was involved in strikes by garment workers in Chicago, New York, and Philadelphia, by brewery workers in Milwaukee, by steel workers in Pittsburgh, by factory workers in New Jersey, and by railroad workers on the west coast. She joined strikers in Canada and worked to organize the miners of Mexico. Wherever the fight was the fiercest, she was there to aid, organize, and encourage. Day and night in poor villages, in tent cities, in lonely cabins, and in crowded ghettoes, she brought solace, defied police lines, used disguises to slip in and out of guarded strike zones, raised funds, and did all she could to make the nation aware of the lonely struggle of the working class.

She remained active until almost the very end of a century of life. When she died on November 30, 1930, a special railway car carried her simple casket to Mount Olive, a little town in the coal fields of southern Illinois. No monuments were erected to commemorate her, but workers knew they were better off because of what she had done.

For more information on her life, see *The Autobiography of Mother Jones*, Arno, 1 New York, 1969.

Absence, watercolour, Elizabeth Bowering

Henry Kaiser 20

"The Amazing Ship Builder"

1882 - 1967

Entrepreneur Henry John Kaiser was born on May 9, 1882, at Sprout Brook, New York. He was one of four children of a shoe factory mechanic and a practical nurse. To help support the family, Henry left school at the age of 13 and worked as a cash boy in a dry-goods store in nearby Utica. Later, he became interested in the photographic supply business and became a travelling salesman, after which he set up his own photographic shop. Subsequently, he opened branches in Miami and Daytona Beach in Florida and Nassau in the Bahamas to catch the tourist trade in the winter. When Kaiser's mother died for lack of medical care, he resolved that someday he would make a contribution towards improving health care services.

In 1906, when he was 24, he fell in love with Bessie Hannah Fosburgh, the daughter of a prosperous businessman. Her father consented to their plans for marriage, under the condition, that Henry meet three requirements within one year; namely, to earn a minimum of $125 a month, to own a house, and to have $1,000 in savings. Believing that the west would offer him better opportunities, Kaiser moved to Spokane, and within a year, he had fulfilled all three conditions. He and Bessie were married in April 1907.

For a few years, he worked for a hardware company, and in 1912, he joined a construction company as salesman and manager of paving contracts. Two years later, he established his first construction enterprise, Henry J. Kaiser Company Ltd. During the next dozen years, he handled millions of dollars worth of highway construction in British Columbia, Washington, Idaho, and California. In 1921, he moved the company headquarters to Oakland, California. Throughout the 1920's, he lived on the road, travelling from one highway paving job to another in his car, his wife at his side, their two sons in the back-seat. With each job, his reputation for efficiency increased. He installed diesel engines in tractors and shovels and built a succession of bulldozers and carryalls. He pleaded with manufacturers for more powerful equipment, and when it wasn't forthcoming, he put it together himself.

When he was 45, he began work on the construction of 200 miles of highway and 500 bridges in Cuba, at a cost of about $20 million. That project required organizing 6,000 workers and fighting serious obstacles, but he completed it within three years. From that experience, he learned the value of teamwork, and in future undertakings, he often formed associations with other contractors for cooperative bidding.

Kaiser's enterprises included laying gas pipelines in the southwestern states and building many dams, bridges, and other engineering works. In 1931, he formed the Six Companies, Inc., which built the Hoover Dam. His approach to this project was to picture in his mind what he wanted and then describe it to one of his artists, who drew the design. His architects then laid out the plans, Kaiser set a date for the construction, and the company began the work and completed it on time. Kaiser was awarded other major contracts as well, including the San Francisco -Oakland Bay Bridge, the Bonneville Dam on the Columbia River, and the Grand Coulee Dam near Spokane. Up to the outbreak of World War II, his company and associate firms had worked on over a thousand projects, totalling $383 million.

In 1939, when he could not find the amount of cement that he needed to construct the Shasta Dam, he established the Permanent Cement Company, building it from the blueprint stage to completion in less than five months. Once the dam was completed, he turned the cement plant over for defence work and supplied all the bulk cement needed to construct Pacific fortifications at Midway, Guam, and other strategic locations.

In 1940, he entered into the shipbuilding industry, building in record time, 60 cargo ships for the British admiralty. Within several months, he was fulfilling contracts from the United States Marines and the Navy. The seven shipyards built and operated by him in California, Oregon, and Washington, produced 1,490 ships, nearly one-third of all American-made merchant ships during World War II. Using mass-production techniques, his workers learned to assemble a prefabricated Liberty ship in less than 10 days. In addition, he built fifty 18,000-ton aircraft carriers. From shipbuilding, Kaiser turned to aircraft construction. He purchased the Fleetwing Aircraft Company of Bristol, Pennsylvania, in 1943 and changed its name to Kaiser Metal Products, Inc. From 1947, in conjunction with Sears Roebuck & Company, Kaiser Metal manufactured kitchen and bathroom ware, as well as, aircraft and missile components.

After the war, Kaiser directed his attention to housing, medical care, and transportation, manufacturing appliances and other household products as well as building over 10,000 houses. One of his proudest achievements, of that period, was his medical plan, begun for his employees in 1942 and made public in 1945. It became the largest privately sponsored health plan in the world. With his wife, he also established the Kaiser Foundation, whose main objective was to bring good medical care within the financial reach of the average person. In 1944, he was awarded the La Salle Medal, and in 1952, he was made a Chevalier of the French Legion of Honour. Throughout his career, he received many honorary degrees.

Kaiser also got involved in the production of postwar steel and in automobile manufacture. He had produced well over a million tons of steel ingots during the war, later increasing his company's capacity to a million and a half tons a year, which amounted to about 45 percent of all the steel produced on the west coast. In 1959, his company doubled its production and became the largest steel producer, west of the Mississippi River. In 1948, Kaiser bought a Ford plant and became the fourth largest producer of automobiles in the United States. In 1953, he turned from pleasure cars to four-wheel drive vehicles when he bought Willys-Overland Motors Inc. He sold his interest to American Motors Corporation in 1969.

In 1954, he began a new building project in Hawaii, and for the rest of his life he lived on the islands, supervising the construction of a hotel, hospitals, plants, housing developments and a $350 million "dream city" called Hawaii Kai.

He died in 1967 at the age of 85.

For more information on his life, see *The Kaiser Story*, published by the Kaiser Industries Corporation, 1968.

North Saskatchewan, watercolour, Sigrid Behrens

Samuel Morse 21

"Painter Turned Inventor"

1791 - 1872

The man, who invented the telegraph and the communications code that bears his name, was born on April 27, 1791, in Charlestown, Massachusetts, the son of a clergyman. He was something of a prodigy and was accepted at Yale University at the age of 14, where he attended lectures on chemistry and electricity. He was also a talented artist, and after graduating from Yale, he wanted to be a painter and to study under Benjamin West in England. The family managed to scrape together the money to send him to Europe where he fulfilled his dream. While in London, he also painted a picture called *The Dying Hercules*, which was judged one of the best of 2,000 works shown at the Royal Academy Exhibition. He made a clay model of the head of Hercules, and on his teacher's advice, had it cast in plaster of Paris and sent it to the Society of Arts. For that work, he received a gold medal.

After four years in England, he returned to the United States and tried to make a living from his paintings but earned very little. He then switched from painting to inventing, helping his brother develop a better water pump. Although their water pump was patented in 1817, it did not bring them any money. Morse travelled from town to town looking for orders for portraits. He received barely enough to feed himself. His luck turned when he met and married Lucretia Walker and went to Charleston, South Carolina for a visit. Word about his portraits got around, and he received many orders earning strong admiration as a portrait painter. This admiration was so strong, in fact, that he was asked to do a portrait of James Monroe, the President of the United States. He sent his family to Connecticut and moved to Washington, D.C.

When his work in Washington was finished, he again travelled the eastern seaboard, now to look for portrait orders for the famous. In what spare time he had, he continued with his other passion, inventing, and came up with a machine for carving marble. He even had the machine manufactured and though it worked perfectly, he couldn't find a market for it. His travels took him to Baltimore where he received a letter from his father advising him that his wife had died. The letter had taken a week to reach him, so that it was too late to attend her funeral. At that time, it crossed his mind that there should be a faster way for people to get in touch with one another.

Leaving his two children with a relative, he moved to New York City to devote all his time to his work. In 1826, he helped form the National Academy of the Arts of Design. He lectured on fine arts, taught young artists, wrote articles on art and science, and continued to paint, yet earned barely enough to support himself and his children. In 1829, when he was 38 and already admired as an excellent portrait painter, he decided to study the paintings of the great masters and journeyed to Italy and France. He lived abroad for three years, but it was not until he was on his way home and became stranded in port for five days, that he took the path that would give him his place in history. Over the dinner table, he and fellow passengers began talking about the extraordinary speed with which electricity could travel across a wire, and he suddenly realized that electricity could be used to send signals at the same speed. He got so excited about the idea that he left the table to pace the deck before sitting down to write his ideas and draw a sketch of an instrument that could do the work. First, he arranged dots and dashes to represent letters and numbers, and then sketched the mechanical details. He could scarcely sleep that night. He worked on his plans the next day and the next, and six weeks later, when the ship reached New York City, he told his brothers of his new invention.

Living with his brother, he worked day and night

trying to perfect his invention. Not only did he have to design every part that would be needed for the machine to operate correctly, he also had to manufacture it himself, since nothing like that was available. After three years of terrible financial struggles, one of his friends managed to get him an appointment as professor of literature at the university. Morse moved into a room near the university and continued his experiments. One of his students heard about the experiments and persuaded his father to help Morse financially. Two years later, Morse was able to give a limited demonstration of his telegraph and gain more support, even receiving a small grant from Congress.

On January 6, 1838, he gave a public demonstration of how his telegraph worked over a distance of three miles. He was then invited to the White House to demonstrate, but some skeptics still maintained that a completely successful telegraph could be invented only by a man of science and not by a painter and teacher. Morse persisted, however, and travelled to England and France to give demonstrations. Within a few years, his telegraph became popular all over Europe, but still, he was having difficulty attracting someone to finance it completely. In 1842, he decided to prove its effectiveness in sending messages through masses of water, so he designed a waterproof cable and had it manufactured and laid underwater for over 100 miles. Then he invited the public and the press to a demonstration, but to his extreme disappointment, the message failed to travel. A later investigation revealed that a boat had been tangled in the cable the previous night and the cable had been cut to free the boat.

At least some of his friends continued to believe in him, in spite of his setbacks, and with their help, he was finally granted $30,000 by the U.S. Congress to build his telegraph. He went to work right away, and on May 26, 1844, he transmitted the results of the Democratic convention from Baltimore to Washington, D.C. He offered his invention to the government for $100,000, but was turned down. He then sold it to private investors, who quickly formed the Western Union Company.

His troubles were not over, however. Several scientists claimed they were the first to invent the telegraph, and Morse had to contend with many lawsuits. Finally, the Supreme Court ruled that the idea was not new, but that he was the first person to put it to practical use. And it continued to prove useful. In 1852, a cable was laid between Great Britain and Ireland, and the next year, Scotland and Ireland and, finally, England and Holland were connected.

In 1856, a cable was laid across the Black Sea. It seemed that only the ocean remained to be crossed by telegraph cable, so in 1857, Morse went to England to help lay a cable across the Atlantic. After several setbacks, the project was finally abandoned. It was picked up again the following year and completed. But just a few days after the cable was down, the telegraph malfunctioned and they had to start over. It was not until 1866 that the first cable carried its messages without any problems.

Morse received many honours and awards and was a guest at one time or another of most of the monarchs and heads of state of the world. He died of pneumonia on April 2, 1872 at the age of 81.

For more information on his life, see *Samuel Morse* by Mona Kerby, F. Watts, New York, 1991.

Ukrainian Ladies, acrylic on canvas, Christina Saruk Reid

Florence Nightingale 22

"Lady with the Lamp"

1820 - 1910

Florence Nightingale, one of the great humanitarians of the 19th century, was born on May 12, 1820 into a very wealthy family. Florence was named for the city where she was born during her parents' four-year honeymoon. She grew up in Hampshire, just north of London, England. She had good looks, an attractive personality, and a fine mind, having been educated largely by her father. Her mother expected her to become a society belle, but Florence did not like parties or idle talk and wanted to be more than a mere socialite.

When Florence was 16, at the time her mother was getting ready to introduce her to the eligible boys in her social circle, she began to hear what she believed was the voice of God telling her that she had a mission. Her mother's thoughts were elsewhere. Feeling that her 15-bedroom house was not adequate for debutante balls, she ordered an extensive renovation and took the family on an 18-month vacation while workers rendered the mansion more suitable. When the family returned, the house was still not ready, so for a few months, they stayed in London, her mother having booked an entire floor of the Carlton Hotel. Although they lived in quiet luxury, Florence longed to help people in need. During her walks, she looked for those who were suffering and often gave them food, clothing, or medicine. Once she spent a few weeks looking after an orphaned baby. She nursed her own grandmother during a serious illness and attended to her grandmother's nurse when she was dying.

What she really wanted was to work in a hospital, but London hospitals, at the time, were notorious for having women of low character as nurses. Consequently, when Florence told her family that she wanted to take up nursing and start a school for training nurses, her mother and sister almost fainted. Her mother tried to persuade her to get married, but Florence flatly refused. She felt that marriage would only make her a social butterfly and obstruct her mission.

In 1844, an American doctor and his wife visited the Nightingales, and Florence shared her dreams with him. Far from trying to talk her out of her plans, the doctor encouraged her. On her own, she read everything she could find on health surveys and hospital care. While travelling, she learned about the Catholic Sisters of Saint Vincent de Paul in Paris and arranged to spend three months in a training school for nurses at Kaisersworth. In 1853, the Institution for the Care of Sick and Gentlewomen in Distressed Circumstances opened a nursing home in London, and she was invited to run it. She gladly accepted the challenge. Later, she used that experience when she took charge of the cholera ward of a big London hospital during an epidemic.

Then the Crimean War erupted, and Florence heard horrifying reports from the front about the aftermath of battle. Recognizing the opportunity to serve, she immediately contacted Sidney Herbert, the Secretary of War. He supported her and arranged for her to take a team of nurses to Scutari. It was not easy to find qualified nurses in those days, but somehow she was able to muster 38, and on October 21, 1854, she and her band of nurses left London with ample supplies of blankets, medicines, food, and linen for bandages.

Even though they desperately needed the help, the army officers did not welcome them, regarding them as young girls meddling in their affairs. The whole hospital was filthy, rats scurried along the walls, and legs and arms were being freely amputated. There wasn't a scrap of proper hospital equipment, nor any plumbing. Men with contagious diseases were laying alongside surgical patients. In the middle of all that lay a dead mule. The doctors were so hostile that her nurses were not allowed in the wards. She man-aged to lend a hand here and there, and within two months, she was virtually running the hospital. She was often on her feet for 24 hours moving from bed to bed, dressing wounds, relieving pain, even writing letters for the soldiers. She made a rule that no one should die alone. Every night, she made a last round of the wards, a quiet figure in a black dress and a white cap, carrying a little Turkish lamp. Soon she became known as the lady with the lamp. But her last months at Scutari were dark. Illness dogged her and on one occasion, only the devoted care of one of her nurses saved her life. The doctors still opposed her efforts, and several nurses had let her down with their quarrels and selfishness. Only the soldiers loved her unequivocally.

By May of 1855, her thoughts turned to the welfare of the British Army at the front. She visited the battlefield and despite her own illness, continued nursing wounded soldiers. By now, reports of her work were all over England, but she did not want any glory, and when the war finally ended, she returned to London under an assumed name to avoid publicity.

In March 1856, she was formally appointed the general superintendent of the female nursing establishment of the military hospitals of the British Army. After a long interview with Queen Victoria, the Queen recommended a royal commission to inquire into health conditions in the army. Florence gave extensive evidence and compiled an immense, confidential report. As a result of that inquiry, the Army Medical School was founded in 1857. In 1860, Florence established the Nightingale School for Nurses, the first of its kind in the world. Within a few years, she was instrumental in opening training schools for midwives and nurses in workhouse infirmaries and played a part in the reform of workhouses.

She continued to be plagued by illness, although no organic disease was ever discovered in her. She stayed in London for the rest of her life, mostly as an invalid. It is widely believed that her illness was partly neurotic and partly feigned. Being an "invalid" left her unable to have a social life of any extent, so she was able to devote herself night and day to whatever task was at hand. Almost single-handily, she raised the profession of nursing to a level of respect and dignity.

In 1907, England's King conferred on her the first Order of Merit awarded to a woman. She died on August 13, 1910 at the age of 90.

For more information on her life, see *Florence Nightingale* by Elspeth Huxley, Weidenfeld & Nicholson, London, 1975.

Psalm 18:2, acrylic on masonite, Wendy Sanchez

Eleanor Roosevelt 23

"The Eyes and Legs of the President"

1884 - 1962

One of America's most beloved philanthropists and advisers to the President, Eleanor Roosevelt began her life politically-connected and the daughter of a wealthy family. Her father was the younger brother of Teddy Roosevelt, the 26th President of the United States. With such a family tree, one would think she would have been off to a good start, but in fact, she was the first child to parents who had been wishing for a boy. Their disappointment became even more evident when they were blessed with two boys after her birth. She was not attractive in any conventional sense. Her mother called her "Granny" because of her looks, and she had to wear a bulky brace on her back to straighten her crooked spine.

Feeling unwanted, she became shy and withdrawn and developed many fears. She was afraid of the dark, afraid of animals, afraid of other children, afraid of strangers, afraid that people would not like her. The only joy in her early childhood was her father, who always cared for her and paid attention to

her. He called her not "Granny," but "Little Golden Hair" or "darling little Nell." But he became an alcoholic, and when Eleanor was only six, he went to live in a sanitarium. She missed him very much and became depressed. Not long afterward, her mother developed painful headaches which did not respond to any treatment. Eleanor rubbed her mother's head for hours, which only seemed to help a little. In spite of this care, her mother died when Eleanor was eight. A few months later, one of her brothers caught diphtheria and also died, and shortly thereafter her father, too, died. Thus, within 18 months she had lost both parents and a brother.

With her remaining brother, she moved to her grandmother's "gloomy, dark townhouse." What she missed the most was that she had no place to play. Her grandmother also inflicted some choice practices on the two children, forcing them to take a cold bath every morning for "health." Eleanor also had to do exercises to help straighten her back, her grandmother making sure that she walked with her arms held behind her, clamped over a walking stick, to improve her posture. Instead of making new friends, Eleanor often sat alone in her room and read. For a long time, she pretended that her father was still alive, and she cherished the letters he had written to her from the sanatorium, letters telling her to be brave and well educated and become a woman who helped the suffering. She often made him the hero of the stories she wrote for her school work.

Just before she turned 15, her grandmother decided to send her to a boarding school in England. The move was a blessing for her. She loved the school, and it's principal and students seemed to like her. She started coming out of her shell, participating in games and socializing. But she was not allowed to complete her education. As soon as she turned 18, her grandmother asked her to come back to "meet people" her age. She always did what she was asked to do, so she returned to the United States.

Back home once more, she was introduced to Franklin Roosevelt, a fifth cousin whom she had met a few times in her childhood. They enjoyed each other's company, meeting secretly at first but soon making their relationship public. On March 17, 1905, they were married. Teddy Roosevelt gave away the bride. In the next 10 years, they had six children, a girl and five boys, one of whom died in infancy. During that time, Eleanor was totally dominated by Franklin's mother who made all the decisions for the family. One of the repercussions of this situation was that the Roosevelts spent far more than they could afford. Eleanor also had marital problems. She did not share her husband's interest in golf and tennis and particularly resented his interest in other women. But she bottled up her anger, and they became more and

more distant. In 1910, Franklin Roosevelt was elected to the New York State Senate, and in 1913, President Woodrow Wilson appointed him Assistant Secretary of the Navy. In spite of their differences, his wife was always at his side to support him.

During World War I, Eleanor Roosevelt threw herself into the war effort, often working 15 or 16 hours a day. She did everything from making sandwiches to knitting sweaters, and she even persuaded the Red Cross to build a recreation room for soldiers who had been shell-shocked in combat.

In the autumn of 1918, she discovered that her husband was having an affair with her social secretary. She offered to divorce him, but he persuaded her to continue with the marriage for the sake of the children and his career. That was the end of all romance in her life, and for the rest of her life, she did what a candidate's wife was supposed to do. She got involved in activities that she liked and ran an independent life, never letting on that she and her husband were not living as a loving couple. When he was struck down by polio in 1921, she supported his quest to remain active in politics, helping him in every possible way during his two terms as Governor of New York and four terms as President of the United States. She became his eyes and legs. She travelled throughout the country. She lectured. She advised him on new legislation. She wrote a regular column entitled "My Day." She answered some of his correspondence.

During World War II, she helped the Red Cross to raise money, donated blood, and sold war bonds. In 1943, she visited barracks and hospitals on islands throughout the South Pacific. When she visited a hospital, she stopped at every bed and had a word with every soldier. Admiral Nimitz, who had been very reluctant to have her at his base, later said, "Nobody else has done so much to help raise the spirits of the men."

When President Roosevelt died on April 12, 1945, she said that perhaps she had pushed him too much, and when he was buried, she visited his grave without fail every day. Later, in December of that year, President Truman invited her to be one of the American delegates to the United Nations. She hesitated, only accepting when the President suggested that it was her duty to do so. In spite of some skeptics' beliefs that she was not qualified for the job, she made enormous contributions to the organization. Almost single-handily, she pushed through the United Nations General Assembly a resolution giving refugees from World War II the right not to return to their native lands if they did not wish to. Next, she helped draft the United Nations Declaration of Human Rights. She insisted that the United Nations should stand for individual freedom, the right of people to free speech, and to the fulfilment of such human needs as health care and education. The Soviet Union and its allies refused to vote on that particular resolution, but it passed by a vote of 48 to zero.

After retiring from her post at the UN, she continued to travel. She dined with presidents and kings, as well as visiting tenement slums in Bombay, factories in Yugoslavia, and farms in Lebanon and Israel. She continued to write her newspaper column and made television appearances. Even as an elderly woman, Eleanor still started her day at 7:30 a.m. and worked until well past midnight. Not only did she continue to write and speak about her favourite causes, but she also actively taught mentally handicapped children and helped raise money for health care for the poor. It is just possible that Eleanor Roosevelt did more for people on a grander scale and for a longer time than any other woman in public life.

She died on November 7, 1962, at the age of 78.

For more information on her life, see *The Story of Eleanor Roosevelt* by Margaret Davidson, Four Winds Press, New York, 1968.

Donalda, watercolour and pencil, Eileen Raucher Sutton

Emily Howard Stowe 24

"Canada's First Female Physician"

1831 - 1903

Born into a southern Ontario Methodist family in 1831, Emily Howard Jennings paved the way for women to become doctors in Canada and was a central figure in Canada's women's suffrage movement.

Being the oldest in a family of six daughters, Emily shared in all household chores yet still found time for her studies. When she was 15, she started teaching in the local school and tried to save money so that she could continue with her own studies. But universities at that time did not accept women, and her only option was to attend the provincial normal school in Toronto for a year. That school was Ontario's first training college for teachers and had been open only six years.

In 1854, at the age of 23, Jennings graduated with a first-class teaching certificate. She was immediately offered a job as principal of the Brantford Public School, about 32 kilometres from her hometown of Norwich. The school was new, and she became the first female school principal in Canada, probably because women at the time were paid half of what a man normally received. By 1870, most of the teachers at the lower grade levels were women.

At the local Methodist Church, she met John Stowe, a carriage-maker, and married him in 1856. She quit teaching to be a homemaker to her husband and three children and for a few years she enjoyed a pleasant family life. But then her husband's health began to fail and doctors told Emily that he was suffering from tuberculosis. To support the family, she took up a teaching position, but as she nursed John, she felt an urge to become a doctor herself. Being a woman was an obstacle, however, because no university in Canada would accept a female medical student, and at that time, there were only three colleges of medicine in the United States that were open to women. But she travelled south, and in 1867, she graduated from the New York Medical College for Women. Her sister looked after her family while she pursued her dream.

When she returned to Canada, the Ontario government refused to give her a license to practice, telling her that she needed to take an additional course, thus putting her up against the University of Toronto's policy not to admit women to the required classes. In 1870, after a great deal of politicking and lobbying, she was finally allowed, to take her course, but it took her another 10 years to receive her license due to "other" requirements which kept mysteriously cropping up. In the meantime, she practiced without a license, while her husband recovered from tuberculosis and studied dentistry. He eventually became a dentist.

In November 1876, Stowe and a group of women organized to fight for women's rights. They called their group the Toronto Women's Literary Guild, choosing that name to avoid being spied on or criticized. They met every Thursday afternoon in the home of one of the members. It was mainly because of their work that the Ontario government passed legislation in 1882 allowing unmarried women who owned property to vote in municipal elections.

Stowe continued to press for the right of women to attend the University of Toronto, Faculty of Medicine, but she was unsuccessful. In 1879 when her daughter Augusta graduated from school, she was accepted by the Victoria Medical School, mainly because its president was a family friend. Augusta thus became the first female medical student in Canada, graduating in 1883. That very year, her mother helped found two medical colleges for women, one in Toronto and another in Kingston. The Toronto school was first called the Women's Medical College, Toronto, but the name was later changed to the Ontario Medical College for Women. Augusta was hired as one of its first instructors. In 1883, Augusta married

Dr. John Benjamin Gullen, and theirs was the first marriage of two Canadian doctors.

In March 1883, Emily Stowe decided to go public and organized an open meeting at Toronto City Hall to form the Toronto Women's Suffrage Association. She kept pressing the University of Toronto to accept women as students until finally, during the 1886-87 session, the university accepted its first female student. However, the medical school was to remain closed to women until 1906.

In 1891, Stowe suffered a great setback when her husband passed away. Two years later, she decided to give up her medical practice and devote all her time to the women's movement. She moved in with her son Frank, next door to Augusta and her husband, and in 1893, organized the Dominion Women's Enfranchisement Association (DWEA). She became its first president, and the following year, they held a national convention. In her role as the president of DWEA, she continued to speak and write about many of the important women's questions of the day.

Stowe was also interested in new religious and political movements, particularly theosophy, a religion based on mysticism. In 1891, she helped start the Toronto Theosophical Society.

She died on April 30, 1903, the day before her 72nd birthday. "Emily" means "industrious," and Emily Stowe spent her entire life trying to live up to that name. Although she did not live long enough to see some of her dreams come true, she was instrumental in the ultimate success of women's suffrage. In 1916, the women of Alberta, Saskatchewan, and Manitoba were granted the right to vote in provincial elections, and in 1918, all women 21 years of age and over won the right to vote in federal elections. Finally, in 1940, women were allowed to vote in Quebec provincial elections. In March 1981, almost 78 years after her death, a postage stamp was issued to recognize her outstanding achievements as a doctor and a suffragist.

For more information on the life of Emily Howard Stowe, see *Emily Stowe,* by Margaret McCallum, Canadian Pathfinders Series, Grolier, Toronto, 1989; or *Emily Stowe: Doctor and Suffragist,* by Mary Beacock Fryer, Hannah Institute and Dundurn Press, Toronto, 1991.

"One person with courage makes the majority"

- Andrew Jackson
President of the United Sates
1829-1837

The Common Thread

To benefit from stories about the lives of others, we need to take ideas from the stories that might help us realize our dreams. Let's see if we can find an answer to the question posed in the introduction: What enables an ordinary person to perform extraordinary feats? Is there one common thread that runs through all 24 stories?

Having read at least a few stories from this collection, you may already have a list of some important traits - confidence, determination, willpower, honesty, urge to serve, persistence. Each of these traits is significant, but are they common to all the stories? If no one trait on your list is present in all of the stories you have read, you may want to add other traits to your list. Is one of them the common thread?

I have studied over 2,000 biographies during the last 10 years. In doing so, I have found that there is one trait that links those who have achieved great things, and I would like to share my findings with you. I believe that the common thread is courage com-

bined with wisdom. I find that no one has ever accomplished anything extraordinary without possessing great courage. Let's look at the role of courage and wisdom in some of the stories in this collection.

Courage enabled Terry Fox to dream of running across Canada on an artificial limb. He had never been much interested in running, except to build his stamina for his basketball games. He had never done any long distance running but after reading the story of the amputee Dick Traum, Fox told himself, " If Dick can run 26 miles, I can run 2,600 miles. Maybe I can even run across Canada. Maybe I can run to raise money for cancer research." Nobody knows exactly what Fox thought on the eve of his amputation, but without any shadow of doubt, I say that it was only his extraordinary courage that propelled him towards his goal. Take away the element of courage and he would have simply vegetated.

It was courage that sustained Mother Jones for nearly 50 years without a family, without a fixed residence, and without a bank account. It was only her extraordinary courage that enabled her to defy the threats from machine guns and prisons. It was also courage that enabled Timothy Eaton to break away from traditional business practices and try to earn a living on his revolutionary ideas in merchandising. If you analysed every single story, you would discover that without courage, the hero or heroine could not have accomplished much.

More than a century ago, Andrew Jackson said, " One person with courage makes the majority." Andrew Jackson knew the role of courage. He was an orphan. Once in his youth, when he refused to polish the shoes of a British officer, he was hit so severely that he sustained a deep scar on his face that remained for the rest of his life. He grew up in the South, which was less loyal to the Union. Yet mainly because of his personal courage, he accomplished the extraordinary feat of becoming President of the United States. If courage can transform a single person into a majority, it can also transform an ordinary person into an extraordinary achiever.

Wisdom is another part of the common thread. Wisdom enables us to determine what is right and what is wrong. Wisdom is acquired mainly through experience, either yours or that of others. Courage without wisdom may be fatal; it takes a type of courage to jump off a high-rise building, but it may not be wise. For healthy development, it is important that both courage and wisdom exist alongside each other.

Great things happen when courage and wisdom meet opportunity. The opportunities that were available to Timothy Eaton, Sanford Fleming, Emily Howard Stowe, or any other extraordinary achiever, were also available to many other persons at the same time. The only reason why these people were able to do something extraordinary was that, that person captured an opportunity that no one else captured.

But how does one capture an opportunity? By using one's wisdom to decide the right course and then having the courage to act on that decision. Failing to make a wise decision at the right moment and then to act on it means missing an opportunity; this is true in every realm of our lives.

People usually know what they have to do to accomplish a goal, however large or small, but only if they possess courage and wisdom can they take the action that is right for them. Everyone knows what it takes to lose weight, but it takes courage and wisdom to take the first step. Everyone knows how to get organized or how to save an hour a day, but it takes courage and wisdom to change one's lifestyle in the way that will benefit oneself the most. Everyone knows how to build a good retirement fund, but it takes courage and wisdom to make financial choices that are right for oneself and then to act on them.

No matter what your current aspirations, there is a good chance that you know how to achieve them, that you know what those first steps are. But it takes a great deal of courage to act on them. I believe that reading biographies can give us courage because regardless of their subjects' immortality in our own minds, we can never forget that they were ordinary people like ourselves who courageously took action when the opportunity presented itself. Terry Fox himself gained the courage to act on his dreams from reading just one small article about a one-legged runner. In the 15 minutes that it took him to read about Dick Traum, Fox became convinced that a one-legged man could participate in a marathon race, and then his courage to act carried him halfway across Canada.

The next chapter provides ideas on how to build courage and wisdom.

Building Courage
& Wisdom

The generation of electrical power begins with a huge reservoir designed to trap billions of gallons of water. There is a turbine at one end of the reservoir and the water, regulated by a control valve, flows into the buckets of the turbine wheel. The weight of the water causes the wheel to turn, and the wheel's motion makes it possible for the electricity to be generated. No matter how much water the reservoir can hold and no matter how great the generator's capability, not even a tiny amount of electricity can be produced until the control valve allows the water to flow into the buckets on the wheel. And, within certain limits, the more the valve is opened, the greater the power that can be generated by the turbines.

We are like the hydraulic power generator. The huge reservoir of water may be compared to the tremendous potential with which we are endowed. Our achievements may be compared to the amount of electricity that the generator can produce and our courage to the control valve in the system. Lack of courage is like a closed control valve. No power can be generated and nothing can be accomplished. A little courage is like a partly opened valve. A little power, a few accomplishments. As our courage is increased, so is our power to achieve, yet with no more potential than we had before. The limit of our achievements is determined not only by the extent of our knowledge, skill, or ability but also by the degree of our courage to express them. As we develop greater courage, we are able to reach more of our potential.

It takes courage to go beyond our known boundaries. It takes courage to try something new or different, especially if we know the whole world is watching. It takes courage to even think of trying something we already believe is impossible. How does one build courage? Here are a few ideas for you to try.

First, read biographies and find out how others overcame the obstacles in their lives. If someone else beat odds similar to yours, you probably can too. Your local library carries a number of biographical books, or you might prefer videos or even programs on public television. All are not only educational but also very effective in building courage and wisdom. You may even want to start your own library of biographies. In that case, your bookstore has a great variety of both individual biographies and compendiums that usually include a number of individuals involved in the same field.

Secondly, join a positive-thinking group. Toastmasters International is an excellent organization in that respect. Their members are always looking for the positive aspects of life's situations and their positive attitudes are contagious. You could also join a volunteer or networking group. Members of these groups are there because they like to reach out to others and to enrich their own lives. By rubbing shoulders with positive people, you can't help but become more optimistic yourself, a great step towards developing courage. Take every opportunity to attend seminars, rallies, and workshops related to building self-confidence, self-esteem, or positive thinking.

Look for a role model that you would like to emulate and then work to develop personal contact with that individual. Just drop a line stating that you see that person as your role model. In most cases, your role model will be impressed by your sincerity and will provide you with more help and guidance than you could imagine.

Take advantage of some of the computer bulletin boards. There you may find a helpful network and/or a vehicle for problem solving.

If you would like additional support, just drop a line to Mentor Communications Inc. It is their mission to help you build courage and wisdom. Through their network, you should be able to connect with people who would love to work with you.

We are on this planet to serve each other. The hand that gives away roses retains some fragrance of the rose. Have the courage to ask for help and/or lend a helping hand.

Your Greatest Legacy

One of our deepest cravings, as humans, is to leave behind some legacy. Some of us strive for wealth, some for a noteworthy reputation, and some for a loving family. One of the greatest legacies you can leave is your life story. How were you raised? What struggles did you have to face? How did you get where you are today? Your children and grandchildren would love to know your story, the way you would tell it, but unfortunately, we often put off talking about the important things we want them to know. Then one day it is too late. You are gone, and they are full of regrets for not delving into your history while they had the chance. If you were to leave behind an account of your life, they would treasure it more than all the wealth and reputation that you might have gained in your lifetime.

Write your story, not for publication or for monetary rewards, but to leave behind a legacy. It is natural for every one of us to down-play our own contributions to our families and our communities, neverthe-

less, our personal histories are both important and interesting. So, spend some time writing a few pages about yourself, whatever you can remember or what is most important to you. It need not be professional; it need only be about you.

Apart from leaving a living testimony for your loved ones, there is another important benefit in writing your story. As you write, you will start taking stock of your achievements, and every accomplishment you log, will boost your self-esteem. At the same time, every misadventure you recount will provide an important caution for others. You will also begin to get a better picture of how you have progressed in your life, which could help smooth your journey into the future and give you a greater appreciation of what you have already accomplished.

Take the courage to write your personal story. Start today.

Profiles of the Artists

SIGRID BEHRENS

Sigrid Behrens was born in Germany and has been a resident of Edmonton since 1954. A member of The Federation of Artists and St. Albert Painter's Guild, Sigrid pursued her art studies at Grant McEwan Community College and the University of Alberta. She has been professionally painting original Alberta landscapes in watercolour since 1988 and has exhibited in various group art shows at Rowles and Parham Design Galleries in Edmonton and Profiles Gallery in St. Albert, Alberta. Her experience of living and travelling in Europe and Canada has given Sigrid a respect for the diversity and beauty of her surroundings, and her watercolours attempt to capture the glorious moods of the Albertan landscape. Her paintings can be found in numerous private and corporate collections throughout Europe, Canada, the United States and, most recently, in China and the Pacific Rim.

BARB BROOKS

Barb Brooks is a multi media artist from Jasper, Alberta. Educated at the University of Washington, Seattle and Montana State University, she studied painting with Manitoba artist, Marcell Debrieul before moving to Jasper in 1976. Alberta Career Development and Employment Board honoured Barb Brooks, in 1992, in their yearly Dream/Dare/Do Program. She also had a successful one woman show in Seoul, Korea as feature international artist at Dankook University in 1993. Conducting workshops for both corporate and private groups as well as for developing artists, the watercolours of Barb Brooks have been included in numerous private and corporate collections all over the world. Barb Brooks has been a feature artist at Rowles and Parham Design Galleries in Edmonton, Alberta since 1987.

ELIZABETH BOWERING

Born in St. John's, Newfoundland, Elizabeth completed her Bachelor's Degree at Memorial University of Newfoundland. From 1988 - 1993, she continued her studies in art at The University of Alberta, Faculty of Extension, Edmonton Art Gallery and SuttonArt. She has participated in various group shows at Johnson's Gallery, Harcourt House, SuttonArt and The Critics Choice Show in Edmonton. In the painting entitled 'Absence' Elizabeth feels that Newfoundlanders' struggle against nature and the elements has always been heroic. The depletion of fish stocks and the recent cod moratorium brings harsh new realities. That which sustained the people even through the leanest of years is just a memory. In this painting, the white of the paper represents the vast, yet empty ocean. The fishing dory, quietly waiting, is symbolic of a proud people unwilling to give up hope. In 'Spanish Charm', Elizabeth was taken by the balcony on this narrow European street filled with history. The living quarters appear cramped and in a state of disrepair, yet rich with the colour and beauty of the balcony flowers.

PHIL DAVIDSON

Born and raised in Ontario, Phil Davidson attended The University of Toronto. He moved to Edmonton as a graduate student and worked at The University of Alberta in research methods and data analysis. However, art and the love of the mountains gradually took over his life. In 1987, he and his wife, painter Eileen Raucher Sutton, opened their own art school in Edmonton, SuttonArt. They enjoy travelling extensively around Western North America, especially hiking Alberta's Rocky Mountains. Associating more with painters than other photographers has made Phil very sensitive to the formal aspects of composition while he explores his own feelings for his subjects. 'Mars Rising' represents a surreal landscape on Sheep Creek, west of Grande Cache: open water almost black in the middle of a February cold snap; strange shapes where the water had overflowed and then had frozen. With no ma-

nipulation in the darkroom, it is a print of what the camera saw.

CECILE DERKATCH

Alberta born, Cecile Derkatch is a watercolour artist who presently resides in Sherwood Park, Alberta. She has completed three years at the University of Alberta Extension and then continued her art studies at SuttonArt for a period of four years. Her affiliations include The Art Society of Strathcona, Wecan Artist Association and The Celebration of Women in the Arts. She was also a volunteer docent with the Edmonton Art Gallery for three years and currently holds a position on the Board of Directors for the Festival Place Cultural Foundation in the County of Strathcona. Represented by several galleries in the Edmonton area, the artwork of Cecile Derkatch can be found in various private and corporate collections. She considers rhythm and flow of pattern to be qualities that guide the eye through her artwork.

KATHERINE FRASER

Katherine Fraser is a resident of Alberta, born in Russia of German parents. Interested in art since she was a young girl, Katherine has studied under numerous instructors at Alberta College of Art, University of Alberta and SuttonArt in Edmonton. She was a finalist for the J.B. Taylor Award for Excellence in Art sponsored by The Medici Art Foundation in 1992. Katherine Fraser takes every opportunity to study people and the human face. "Quadra Island Woman" is an example of her skill in painting portraits. Her artwork can be found in many private collections.

HERMAN GOIGNER

Herman Goigner was born in Austria in 1944 and has been a resident of Alberta since 1970. Graduating from the University of Calgary in 1977 with a B.A. in history and

Political Science, Herman worked extensively in the hotel industry and developed an interest in the arts as a volunteer docent and library assistant at the Edmonton Art Gallery. He pursued art studies at SuttonArt from 1988 to the present. He has exhibited his paintings since 1989. His chosen medium is acrylic; the method of application is spontaneous - broad sweeping brush strokes express an inner release as well as a strong identification with a specific place or scene.

ANDREA HOUSE

Andrea House was born in Fort St. John, British Columbia and presently resides in Edmonton, Alberta. She is in her third year at the University of Alberta, at the Faculté St. Jean. She has also been studying art for five years at SuttonArt. She has been involved in various student shows at SuttonArt, Phoenix Theatre in Edmonton and in Dijon, France. The painting of the cityscape of Montreal came from a recurring dream that Andrea had after leaving the city. In her work, she explores dream-like qualities of her subject matter. She is fascinated by iconography and enjoys mixing unusual elements to create a strong subtext within the painting.

YURIKO IGARASHI KITAMURA

Yuriko Kitamura was born in Hokkaido, Japan and obtained her BSc. in 1963. After immigrating to North America, she began to experiment with various art forms through courses at the University of Alberta and the Metchosin International Summer School of the Arts in Victoria, British Columbia. Her paintings on rice paper and silk create a unique expression. Represented by various galleries in Western Canada, she has been involved with a large number of solo and group shows from 1986 to the present, as well as being featured in various articles and publications in Edmonton and Japan. Her attraction to two divergent aspects of nature, the powerful grandeur of mountains and the delicate beauty of the flower, led her to the development of her own technique of dye painting. Her art work has been included in various public and private collections throughout North America, England and Japan.

RENEE LAFONTAINE

Born in Yorkton, Saskatchewan, Renee Lafontaine moved to Edmonton in 1970. She has studied various aspects of painting under the instruction of Ihor Dymitruk, Chuck Hughes, Eileen Raucher Sutton, Christina Saruk Reid and Frank Haddock. She has participated in several group shows at SuttonArt, Cafe de Ville, Strathcona Art Society and The Works Festival in Edmonton, Alberta. She has become extremely interested in the numerous festivals and parades that take place in Edmonton and has concentrated on portraying their excitement on canvas. In the acrylic paintings entitled "Fringe Benefits" Renee captures the colour and atmosphere of the annual Fringe Festival in Edmonton.

MOLLY MACISAAC

Molly MacIsaac has lived in Edmonton since 1976. Her background began in graphic arts and portraiture. Her experience has covered several mediums, but she always returns to her first love, watercolour. Concentrating on developing a style and technique in high realism, she has been commissioned widely by various corporations and her paintings can be found in corporate collections throughout the world. One hallmark of her artistry is her vivid attention to detail and to setting a mood in her work through the use of high contrast of light and dark. The artwork of Molly MacIsaac has been represented by Rowles and Parham Design Galleries in Edmonton since 1986 and in several galleries in Ottawa, Ontario.

NATASHA MANELIS

Born in Tadzhikistan, Russia, Natasha Manelis is a watercolour artist living in Edmonton, Alberta. She graduated from the Art College of Tadzhikistan in 1990 and from St. Petersburg Fine Arts Institute, Department of Painting, Glass and Pottery in the spring of 1993. Natasha came to Canada in late spring of 1993. She has exhibited her artwork in several galleries in St. Petersburg, Karelia (a Republic of Russia), in Finland and at Rowles and Parham Design Galleries in Edmonton, Alberta. She describes her style of painting as Leningrad post modernist and includes both interiors and exteriors in most of her paintings. Although they belong to the same world, one's interior space is subjective and reflects individual choice. The delicate and original nature of her paintings is enhanced by an elegant style and expression of colour.

WAYNE MCGALE

Wayne McGale was born in Waco, Texas into a Canadian Armed forces family who spent time in several centres around North America. In 1970, he settled in Edmonton, where he currently resides. Wayne has loved to draw for as long as he can remember. Since 1975, schizophrenia has made dealing with mundane reality a struggle, but his life within his visual imagination is exceptional. Wayne's output consists mainly of pencil and ink drawings spanning a wide range of themes. After a few minutes studying the work of a master artist, he has incorporated the style; never copying the style, let along any specific piece, but nonetheless demonstrating a direct visual comprehension. Wayne studied for two years with Eileen Raucher Sutton at SuttonArt. The painting, Headmaster, is not about any individual; it expresses an intuitive, general interpretation of an aspect of some people. Wayne rarely titles his pieces; they speak visually.

BILL MILLER

Bill Miller's personal journey has been one of extremes. Born in Edmonton, Alberta, forty seven years ago, Bill's life evolved around his natural athletic abilities that led him to a semi -professional level. In 1980, a diagnosis of Multiple Sclerosis moved Bill's journey in a dramatically different direction. What was an emphasis on the physical became a journey of self discovery directed to his spiritual side. With his diagnosis, he developed a renewed connection to artistic expression and the compelling need to document his journey. This one time designer/architectural illustrator became an expressionistic painter, poet and teacher. As the journey continues to a point where Bill requires assistance for all his personal physical needs, his abilities to produce paintings and poetry have come to the fore. In the watercolour entitled 'Deja Vu', Bill believes that the artist becomes the vehicle motivated from within and guided by the spirit of art.

JO PETTERSON

Alberta born, Jo Petterson completed a Bachelor of Education at the University of Alberta and has participated in various group shows in Edmonton, Leduc and Red Deer. Jo has had a one person show at the Leduc Civic Centre in Leduc. About the painting entitled "Making Memories", Jo explains "It is comforting and peaceful to enjoy the pond with my dad, recognizing every line of his structure, the relaxed slope of his shoulders, the slight lean in his stance, the familiar smell of his clothes and the gentle squeeze of his strong hand around my small fingers. We watch the ducks together, toss them bits of bread and marvel at their agility in the water. The memory becomes the moment. Now I see the warm familiarity of my Dad's back. And I see my eager son where I once stood. This is a painting of love past...present...and forever.

CHRISTINA SARUK REID

Born and raised in Alberta, Christina received a Bachelor of Fine Art and a Bachelor of Education from the University of Alberta in 1982 and 1990 respectively. She graduated with a Master in Fine Art from the School of the Arts Institute of Chicago in 1985. Involved in both group and solo shows since 1988, Christina has exhibited in Alberta, Ontario, as well as Chicago, Detroit and in Gainsville, Florida. She was a participant in a show entitled "Cross Ties", that toured six artist run centres across Canada. Her publications include the Alberta Advisory Council, Women's Issue Annual Report, Alberta Psychology Magazine and "Borderlands" 'Art of the Edge'. She has worked as a corporate consultant, instructor and illustrator for various associations. Christina draws on her own or other's life experience in her paintings and uses the formal elements, ie. colour and composition, to emphasize the personalities of the people she paints.

ADELINE ROCKETT

Born in Saskatchewan and a resident of Edmonton since 1969, Adeline Rockett received her B.A. and B.Ed. from the University of Saskatchewan and an M.Ed. from the University of Alberta. Her affiliations include the Canadian Society of Painters in Water Colour and the Alberta Society of Artists. A landscape painter working in watercolours and acrylics, Adeline is a recipient of several prestigious awards. In 1982, she was an award winner in the Canadian Society in Water Colour, 57th Annual Juried show. In 1983, she won the Husky Oil Award in 'Art Alberta', and in 1984 she was the recipient of the Petro Canada Award. Adeline has been included in numerous publications and catalogues. She has had 35 solo shows and her work is included in over seventy corporate and public collections throughout North America and Europe including the Royal Collections of Drawings and Watercolours at Windsor Castle in England.

She was also one of 25 Canadian artists chosen to represent Canada in 'International Waters', a show that toured Canada, the United States and the United Kingdom from 1991 to 1993.

WENDY SANCHEZ

Wendy Sanchez was born in Vancouver and resides in Sherwood Park, Alberta. She has a varied education that includes Manitoba College of Art, The Ontario College of Art, Mt. Allison University in New Brunswick, University of Alberta under the instructors Paul Braid and Alfred Schmidt, portrait painting under Esther Freeman and developmental painting under the instruction of SuttonArt. She has been represented by various galleries in the Edmonton area and was commissioned to complete fourteen large murals ranging from 5 to 88 feet in length for Mills Haven Elementary School in Sherwood Park. Her acrylic paintings have been included in various public and private collections in North America, Greece, Spain, Germany and England. She enjoys creating large paintings that fill a room and that project a feeling of strength, peace and beauty.

EILEEN RAUCHER SUTTON

Born and raised in New York City, Eileen Raucher Sutton received both her Bachelors and Masters Degrees in Fine Art from City University of New York. She showed extensively in the New York area and received acclaim from such prominent critics as Lawrence Alloway, the most important critic in several decades; Ann Percy, curator at the Philadelphia Museum of Art; and Linda Shearer, assistant curator of the Guggenheim Museum. Her work hangs in numerous corporate and private collections throughout North America. After teaching in the school system in New York for several years, Eileen ran her own school there for eight years, until she moved to Edmonton in 1984. She and her husband, photographer Phil Davidson, now run their school, SuttonArt in Edmonton. Though her large watercolour florals and landscapes appeal to a broad audience, Eileen's figure drawings are much appreciated by connoisseurs for their very direct, uncluttered expression. Eileen has been drawing from models weekly for over two decades and considers the experience an essential discipline for serious artists.

VIVIAN THIERFELDER

Born in Alberta in 1949, Vivian Thierfelder received a B.F.A. in Visual Arts from the University of Alberta, and though having worked successively in oils, acrylics and egg tempera, she now concentrates solely on the demands of watercolour realism. Her works are noted for rich colour and textural treatment, along with a love of illuminated detail, producing a remarkable visual clarity. Elected a member of the Canadian Society of Painters in Water Colour in 1983, Vivian has been participating in solo and group shows in Edmonton, Victoria, Dallas, New York City, Chicago, Toronto and Vancouver. A collection of six of her original watercolours have been featured in the book entitled 'From The Garden' by Judy Schultz in 1993. Her artwork is included in both public and private collections throughout the world.

ELAINE TWEEDY

Raised on a farm in the Ardrossan district, Elaine was born in Edmonton, Alberta and currently resides in Leduc, Alberta. There has been a long history of artistic talent among family members. Elaine has studied under numerous professional artists including Eileen Raucher Sutton and Gisela Felsberg of Edmonton. Since 1988, Elaine has participated in various group shows through the Federation of Canadian Artists and Red Deer & District Museum with several solo exhibitions at the Leduc Civic Centre. Elaine enjoys bringing her favourite subjects to life in oils, acrylics and water-

colours and has been particularly inspired by the painting 'en plein -air'. The painting of Johnson Lake was captured on location in Banff National Park and received the Jean Stephenson Scholarship Award in 1993 from the Alberta Arts Clubs Association. The artwork of Elaine Tweedy can be found in various private and corporate collections.

For more information about the artwork or artists in this book or for information about purchasing artwork please call:

Mentor Communications Inc.
(403) 429-6342 or 1-800-4-MENTOR

Mission Statement

MENTOR COMMUNICATIONS INC.

"Helping you build courage and wisdom"

Acknowledgment

A project like *24 Heroic Journeys* could not have come about without the support and help of many people. Thanks to all those who encouraged us to keep the project moving along, and to the editors and reviewers, who provided their time and energy.

And especially to

Ravi Bakshi, of Miracom, for his support and technical magic in making computer programs understand each other. We did not mean to bother him as much as we did and appreciate his patience and expertise.

Phil Davidson from SuttonArt for reacting so quickly to our request for artwork and for his exceptional skill in photographing the artwork that was eventually selected.

Era Rowles of Rowles and Parham Design Galleries, who provided total support throughout the entire project's life on each level of its development. This project would not have gone ahead without Era's consultation and expertise and the support work that she and her gallery staff provided.

Rod Peden, of the law firm Jomha Peden, for his legal advise, support, friendship and humourous antidotes during our lunches together.

Dan Hardie, for stepping up to the plate and handling the layout and design for the book and magically putting all the pieces together.

And finally

In the early stages of the project, a chance meeting linked us with a man in a wheelchair, who provided the initial concept of the book format and later assisted in the selection of the artwork. That man's name is **Bill Miller**. We used one of Bill's art pieces (see page 50) in the book. An extraordinary achiever, Bill spends his time painting, helping, guiding others and fostering the concept of mentoring on a daily basis. Despite the fact that Bill has Multiple Sclerosis and is confined to a wheelchair, he provided the inspiration and the determination necessary to get the project off the ground and to fruition.

Mentor Communications Inc. salutes Bill for his vital contribution in this project.